Water Gardening

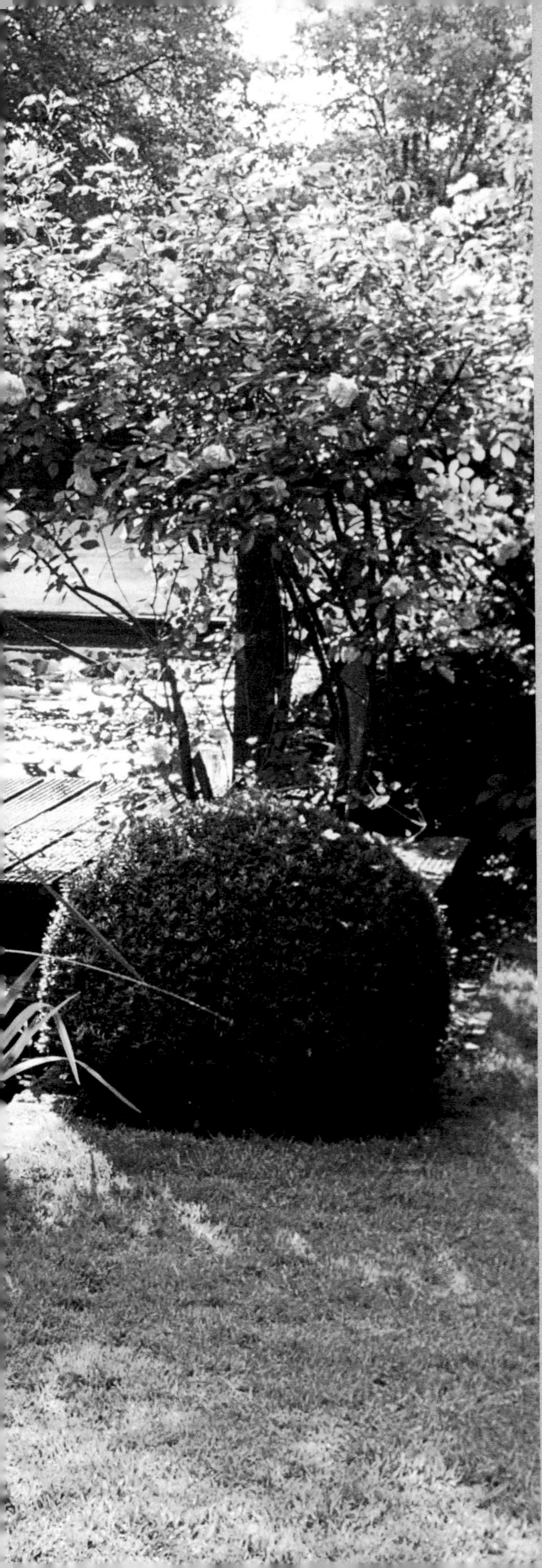

Alan Titchmarsh
how to garden

Water Gardening

BBC BOOKS

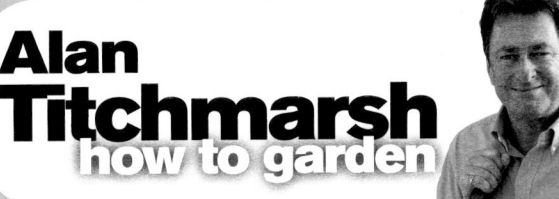

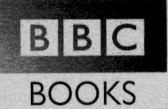

10 9 8 7 6 5 4 3 2 1

Published in 2013 by BBC Books, an imprint of
Ebury Publishing, a Random House Group Company

The Random House Group Limited
supports The Forest Stewardship Council
(FSC®), the leading international forest
certification organisation. Our books
carrying the FSC label are printed on
FSC® certified paper. FSC is the only
forest certification scheme endorsed by
the leading environmental organisations,
including Greenpeace. Our paper
procurement policy can be found at
www.randomhouse.co.uk/environment

FSC
www.fsc.org
MIX
Paper from
responsible sources
FSC™ C004592

A CIP catalogue record for this book is available from
the British Library.

ISBN 978 1 84 990223 6

Produced by OutHouse!
Shalbourne, Marlborough, Wiltshire SN8 3QJ

BBC BOOKS
COMMISSIONING EDITOR: Lorna Russell
PROJECT EDITOR: Nicholas Payne
PRODUCTION: Rebecca Jones

OUTHOUSE!
COMMISSIONING EDITOR: Sue Gordon
SERIES EDITOR & PROJECT EDITOR: Polly Boyd
SERIES ART DIRECTOR: Robin Whitecross
CONTRIBUTING EDITOR: Jo Weeks
DESIGNERS: Heather McCarry, Louise Turpin
ILLUSTRATIONS by Lizzie Harper, Susan Hillier,
Janet Tanner
PHOTOGRAPHS by Jonathan Buckley except where
credited otherwise on page 96
CONCEPT DEVELOPMENT & SERIES DESIGN:
Elizabeth Mallard-Shaw, Sharon Cluett

Colour origination by Altaimage, London
Printed and bound by Firmengruppe APPL,
Wemding, Germany

Contents

Introduction

Gardening is one of the best and most fulfilling activities on earth, but it can sometimes seem complicated and confusing. The answers to problems can usually be found in books, but big fat gardening books can be rather daunting. Where do you start? How can you find just the information you want without wading through lots of stuff that is not appropriate to your particular problem? Well, a good index is helpful, but sometimes a smaller book devoted to one particular subject fits the bill better – especially if it is reasonably priced and if you have a small garden where you might not be able to fit in everything suggested in a larger volume.

The *How to Garden* books aim to fill that gap – even if sometimes it may be only a small one. They are clearly set out and written, I hope, in a straightforward, easy-to-understand style. I don't see any point in making gardening complicated, when much of it is based on common sense and observation. (All the key techniques are explained and illustrated, and I've included plenty of tips and tricks of the trade.)

There are suggestions on the best plants and the best varieties to grow in particular situations and for a particular effect. I've tried to keep the information crisp and to the point so that you can find what you need quickly and easily and then put your new-found knowledge into practice. Don't worry if you're not familiar with the Latin names of plants. They are there to make sure you can find the plant as it will be labelled in the nursery or garden centre, but where appropriate I have included common names, too. Forgetting a plant's name need not stand in your way when it comes to being able to grow it.

Above all, the *How to Garden* books are designed to fill you with passion and enthusiasm for your garden and all that its creation and care entails, from designing and planting it to maintaining it and enjoying it. For more than fifty years gardening has been my passion, and that initial enthusiasm for watching plants grow, for trying something new and for just being outside pottering has never faded. If anything I am keener on gardening now than I ever was and get more satisfaction from my plants every day. It's not that I am simply a romantic, but rather that I have learned to look for the good in gardens and in plants, and there is lots to be found. Oh, there are times when I fail – when my plants don't grow as well as they should and I need to try harder. But where would I rather be on a sunny day? Nowhere!

The *How to Garden* handbooks will, I hope, allow some of that enthusiasm – childish though it may be – to rub off on you, and the information they contain will, I hope, make you a better gardener, as well as opening your eyes to the magic of plants and flowers.

Introducing water gardens

Water will transform a garden, bringing it magically to life. It has many assets, but perhaps its greatest is its versatility. Whatever the size of your outdoor space, there are water features to suit the situation, from tiny wall spouts to exuberant fountains and from half-barrel pebble pools to large wildlife ponds. There are neat, geometric designs for formal gardens and sinuous ones for informal plots. This section looks at the options, helping you choose a water feature to suit your needs, style preferences and garden layout.

Why have water?

Whether we're on a trip to the seaside, having a picnic by a river or relaxing beside a bubbling stream, most of us enjoy being near water. Our attraction to it may be because it's essential to life, but surely it's also because of its beguiling qualities. In the garden, water brings shimmering areas of light and stimulating or soothing sounds, creating a vibrant or calm atmosphere and a strong sense of being closer to nature.

Design benefits

Water is tremendously versatile and can be used in many ways to create a variety of effects. It fits into any space – effortlessly complementing plants and hard landscaping – and can be integrated into an existing design or used as the central theme for a new garden. For instance, if you want a natural-looking garden where water predominates, you can surround your pond with lush, damp-loving plants, then extend this 'bog' into an informal, wild area, perhaps crossed with a timber walkway. Alternatively, a small pond tucked in a corner backed by shrubs and trees will create the feel of a woodland glade. For a bit of glamour, a formal pool surrounded by polished hard landscaping and simple, bold planting can capture the essence of a Californian-style garden.

Using water at different levels

Unlike most garden features, water can be used at any level – from a sunken pond to a fountain that sprays way above your head. Water can be used to accentuate the horizontal or the vertical plane, offering a wealth of exciting design opportunities. For instance, where a garden has been created on several levels, a 'natural' stream with one or more waterfalls or a cascade can be made to link them, emphasizing the change in height and creating visual interest (*see* page 17). In a more formal design, or on a patio, two square or rectangular ponds – one raised above the other and with a connecting water spout – would work well (*see* page 18). A traditional freestanding two-tier pool fountain (*see* page 16) also looks the part, particularly in a courtyard.

Focal points

Water is perfect for creating focal points, and fountains are an obvious choice. A simple raised pool with a lively fountain demands attention at the far end of a path or in the centre of a garden 'room'. Water can also be used to highlight a specific area or to redirect your gaze from less pleasing views. Sometimes a group of identical smaller features, such as birdbaths, urns or copper funnels, can be effective. Arranged in a row of three, they will take your eye along a path or through an archway.

Don't forget

Water is beneficial for the time-pressed gardener; most water features, once installed, are relatively low-maintenance.

The square shape of this pond lends an air of formality to the garden, while the varied planting around the edges softens the straight lines of the paving and creates a relaxed feel.

Reflective qualities

Still water is calm and tranquil, but never lifeless. Its minutely disturbed surface is beautifully reflective, creating endless plays between light and shadow. The sky and clouds reflected in a pool increase the feeling of space and provide a sense of movement in a garden, while the reflections of plants around its edge can give the impression of denser planting and greater water depth.

Even a tiny body of still water, such as a birdbath or bowl (*see* page 19), has plenty of uses. Positioned in a bright spot, its water will reflect light onto dark walls or plants nearby. In a more shaded area, its shiny surface attracts the eye from a distance, while its reflection creates the illusion of greater space.

Surrounded by a variety of leafy architectural plants, this waterfall makes an elegant feature; the cascading water looks magnificent and sounds wonderfully refreshing.

The reflective qualities of water have been used to good effect in this simple pool, which acts as a calm space within the hard landscaping.

Sound

Moving water of any sort is irresistibly eye-catching, and the noise that it makes is another of its many attractions.

Different water features make different sounds: a pebble pool gently pulses, a fountain rises and falls, a waterfall gushes and tumbles. A slow but variable trickle can be mesmerizing and calming, as can uniform bubbling, while the noise of faster water is more invigorating. Any of these can be used to enhance your garden, depending on the effect you want to create. A louder, watery noise is excellent for blocking out intrusive background sounds (such as traffic), while a gentle, intermittent drip might be the ideal choice for a serene pool set in a quiet location with a comfortable bench nearby.

Wildlife

Water is always a magnet for wildlife, which is enjoyable both for its own sake and for its positive impact on the whole garden. Almost any size of water feature will attract wildlife. Water boatmen, damselflies and dragonflies are among the first to arrive, but it's amazing how frogs and newts seem to sense a new pond in the vicinity and appear from nowhere. Birds drink and bathe in water, and at night hedgehogs will visit for a refreshing draught. It's always a good idea to put a seat near a pond for wildlife-watching, and you could consider extending an area of decking to create a viewing platform.

As well as being a pleasure, having wildlife in the garden is helpful to

A sunny position, gently sloping edges, pebble sides and varied planting, including some native wildflowers, help make this pond irresistible to wildlife.

the gardener: the creatures consume many garden pests, including slugs and snails, and you also have the satisfaction of knowing that you've provided them with a habitat, so helping their survival. For more on wildlife ponds, *see* pages 40–1.

Fish

For many people, fish go hand in hand with a pond, and there's no denying they add interest. It is amazing just how much time can be spent watching them flit around in the cool depths doing not very much at all, and it's great fun feeding them, too. Goldfish and their more showy relations are a good choice and are fairly easy to care for (*see* pages 58–9). Koi carp are more demanding and need their own filtration system; they can also be destructive to submerged plants.

Goldfish are well suited to an ornamental pond and always grab your attention. Water lilies seem to be their perfect companions.

Pond styles

If you're going to create a pond from scratch, it's vital to spend some time before you start work thinking about the styles that appeal to you and will suit your garden. Essentially, there are two styles – informal and formal – but there are many variations. Consider the practicalities as well as the end result.

Informal ponds

Informal ponds can be any shape, but they are usually sunk into the ground (see pages 34–7) and made to look as natural as possible. They are also quite densely planted, which encourages wildlife. This in turn helps to create a well-balanced ecosystem, which will make the pond more or less self-sustaining. Most naturalistic ponds require only a minimal amount of maintenance.

Informal ponds suit country or cottage-style gardens, or those that have a seaside or jungle theme, but they will also fit happily in an urban garden, even a semi-formal one.

Waterfalls, streams and cascades all enhance the natural effect, as do banks, islands, stepping stones and pebble 'beaches' (see pages 14–15, 40 and 50–1).

Curved shapes

A pond that has a gently curving outline looks comfortable in most situations. It can be sited beside features with straight lines or curves, such as flower beds, paths, a patio or seating area, and it can sit in a corner or to one side of the garden, at the foot of a slope, or around a natural promontory within the garden. The size of a curved pond can easily be adjusted to fit into the site without spoiling its overall appearance, and it doesn't matter if the curves are slightly out of kilter because the whole thing is intended to look relaxed. Most informal ponds do not end up with a clear outline anyway, simply because the whole idea is to blur the pond edges with planting or natural landscaping materials. Curved ponds are the best choice when it comes to creating a bog garden alongside a pond (see pages 42–3).

Regular shapes

Although an irregularly curved outline is the most obvious choice for an informal garden, there's no reason not to have a square, rectangular, oval or round pool. This can be particularly useful in small gardens, where space is at a premium, or those where the surroundings determine the shape to a greater or lesser extent. For example, a courtyard garden will generally look best with a square, rectangular or hexagonal pond. Setting the pond in the corner, rather than centrally, and softening and disguising the edges with planting, will help to give it an informal look.

With lush foliage plants around its edge and a carefully sited bench, this informal pond provides a great temptation to sit and enjoy the scene.

Don't forget

Curved ponds are the easiest to build. They are simple to lay out, dig and waterproof, using a flexible liner (see pages 34–6).

Formal ponds

Formal, or ornamental, ponds may be raised or sunken and are designed to act as a distinct decorative feature within a garden, such as a focal point. If you have a simple, modern or minimalist garden, a formal pond is the best choice. Small, raised ponds are particularly effective and are also good where space is restricted (*see* pages 38–9).

With formal ponds, the emphasis is on shape (usually geometric) and architectural qualities, rather than plants. So the edges, paths and other hard landscaping features around the pond are often just as important as the water. Adding a fountain or statue with a water spout is the traditional way to ensure the pond is eye-catching, but a body of still water can be equally attractive.

Unlike informal ponds, formal ponds usually have only one or two types of plant – often water lilies and, for contrast, perhaps a plant with spiky, upright foliage. Ornamental fish are often seen in formal ponds.

Formal pond shapes

A square or rectangular pond will accentuate or echo the straight lines of a building or the hard landscaping. It will also complement formal planting, such as neatly clipped hedges or a traditional-style rose garden.

Circles are good for creating a formal look too: round ponds sit comfortably with circular or semi-circular patios or lawns, for instance. On the other hand, they can also help to soften the rigidity of straight lines while retaining the formal feeling of a space.

A simple shape and white bricks contrasting with a dark inner liner ensure that this formal pool introduces a feeling of calm among its lively surroundings.

Positioning formal ponds

You can't hide a formal pond in a corner or smother it in vegetation. It must be given an open position, with nothing to spoil the look of the water or the clean symmetry of the pond's shape. Alternatively, you could create a garden 'room' especially for it, adding the hard landscaping and plants at the same time for a cohesive look.

A flat site is usually easiest for a formal pond, but a slope offers the chance to have a split-level pool with linking waterfalls.

Construction and upkeep

Formal ponds, whether raised or sunken, need to be constructed meticulously, as symmetry and perfection are vital – they are not as forgiving as informal ponds. Check all corners are at right angles and that the ground and top are level.

A good ecosystem is less likely to develop where there are few plants and non-native fish, so you will probably have to install a pump and filter (*see* pages 32–3) to keep the water clean and healthy. A formal pond requires regular maintenance, and you will need to spend time keeping it neat and tidy – a prerequisite of such a feature.

Don't forget

Squares instantly create a sense of formality. Adding square stepping stones to a shallow rectangular water feature is a simple way to introduce interesting areas of light and dark.

To make the most of your water feature, you need to integrate it into the rest of your garden so it looks like it belongs. Plants, paths, patios and other seating areas are all important, but you can also add features that are specific to the water itself and will add to your enjoyment. These include banks, islands and stepping stones, bridges and walkways. Choose styles that are appropriate for your style of pond or stream and your garden as a whole.

Banks, contours and terraces

One of the easiest ways to get rid of the spoil from making a pond or water feature is to use it to create a bank or reshape existing contours in a garden.

Steep banks look best beside natural ponds and streams and in gardens where there are already changes of level. Shallower mounds with gently sloping sides can be effective in flat sites, especially to contour the ground around the pond so that it looks as if it is in a natural hollow in the garden. Careful surrounding planting will disguise the edges.

In a formal garden, the spoil can be used to create terraces and steps around a central sunken pool. Edged with walls of bricks, stone or rendered concrete blocks, these will emphasize the formality of the pool area.

Islands

Because of its inaccessibility, an island adds an air of seclusion or even mystery. Depending on its size, it will also provide a safe retreat for wildlife.

A basic island is easy to make. Line the pond as normal, then, before filling it, build the island using bags of sand. Arrange these to make the shape required and fill the hollow centre with soil for planting. With complex shapes, you may need to line the centre with hessian to ensure the soil stays put. Check your levels to ensure the bags

The finishing touches are what make a pond really special.
① Lush planting on a semi-formal bank.
② A simple natural grassy island.
③ Slightly raised stepping stones are just asking to be followed through a stream.

will be hidden when the pond is filled with water. It's a good idea to use hessian bags for the top layer, because the plants will be able to spread their roots into them so they become less obvious. Check the sandbags regularly and replace them before they rot.

In a formal pond, the island often looks best when it has a regular, geometric shape. For example, placing a square or perfectly circular island in the centre of a square pool produces a pleasingly minimalist pattern. Use spiky architectural plants to keep the edges sharp. This type of island needs careful

Don't forget

An island will need some maintenance, so make sure you can reach it safely when the pond is full.

planning to work well, but can be very effective in the right setting.

Stepping stones

There is something irresistible about stepping stones: both adults and children are drawn to them, and it takes a strong will to resist crossing them to find out what's on the other side. Stepping stones across a stream or shallow pond, or through a bog garden, will ensure it's part of any walk in the garden. Set them close together or a leg-stretch apart; they can be staggered or make a straight path.

Depending on the material used, stepping stones can look at home in any pond. In a formal setting with a straight-edged pool, rectangular or square stones will underline the formality, while round or free-form stones will introduce a light-hearted touch. A winding line of flat-topped stones across a shallow point in a stream will give it a natural look.

To fit stepping stones across a pond, build wide-based piers on the liner, protecting it with liner offcuts, then mortar the paving slabs to the piers. Alternatively, put stepping stones around the pond, or through a surrounding flower bed or bog garden.

Walkways and bridges

Timber walkways, or boardwalks, can be used in a similar way, to enable you to cross or walk beside water or boggy areas. Their straight lines look appropriate beside modern, formal pools, but they can also be more rustic in appearance, winding slowly through seaside-style marshes with tall grasses on either side, or over bog gardens full of lush plants. Rough-hewn fencing posts add to the natural effect.

Unlike a walkway, which should appear to stretch on without a distinct end, a bridge has a start and a finish and often has at least a slight arch in the middle. A bridge is good for ensuring the water feature is included

in a walk around the garden, but it should look as if it is serving a purpose, not simply ornamental. Bridges can be used to link separate pools, to give the effect of a larger body of water; conversely, they can be used to break up a large expanse.

To cross a natural-looking stream or pond, a simple timber bridge will look best. Use grooved decking board or old railway sleepers covered in chicken wire to make a non-slip surface. Decking board is just as good a choice in a contemporary-style garden, or you can make a bridge-like structure with brick, stone or rendered concrete.

Japanese-style bridges, traditionally painted red, make good focal points in a semi-formal setting where paths and hard landscaping play a conspicuous role. In an informal or minimalist garden, they tend to look out of place.

Water crossings are inviting and always improve a water garden.

① A wooden bridge over a bog garden is both practical and provides visual interest.

② A timber walkway extends from the deck and divides the water feature.

Don't forget

Ready-made garden bridges are popular. They come in many different designs – with or without handrails, arched or almost flat.

Moving water

There is nothing quite like the sound and sight of water to bring life into a garden, but it can also increase the sense of tranquillity, depending on the way in which it is used. A feature with moving water can be fun or serious, flamboyant or discreet. The biggest challenge is when you want it to look as though it is completely natural – but even this can be achieved with a bit of careful work.

Fountains

Of all the types of moving water features, fountains are the most varied and probably most popular; they create a showy water display and produce a pleasing sound. One of their great benefits is that they're easy to install and can be added to a pond or rill; all you need is a pump with a fountain attachment. If you don't have space for a pond, you can install a freestanding, self-contained fountain (*see* page 20).

Fountains do not make a pretence of looking natural, nor do they blend into the landscape, so the key is to match yours to the style of the water feature and your garden. A few of the most familiar types of standard-sized fountain are described here, but there are many other small, low fountains, including spouts and pebble fountains – ideal for tiny spaces (*see* pages 19–21).

Spray fountains

There is a wide variety of spray patterns; choose one that produces the effect you want to achieve. Plume fountains produce jets of water out of a hole or holes in the top of a fountainhead. The plumes project into the air, and their height can be altered to suit the size of the pond. Many pumps allow the flow to be adjusted from steady to various pulsing intervals. A single steady plume fountain looks particularly good in a raised formal pond, where it will act as a focal point.

Often used in smaller pools, some spray fountains produce a thin film of water shaped like an inverted bell; the low, rounded 'curtains' of water create little disturbance to the surface. These bell-shaped fountains look best in a formal or modern-style pool, positioned well away from any planting.

The water from this bubbling two-tier fountain will cascade into a small shallow pool at its base.

Narrow jets of water form an eye-catching, multi-tiered fountain at the centre of this rectangular pond.

Don't forget

Most pond pumps come with a range of fountainheads and variable pressure settings, which allow you to alter the appearance of the water flow and the sound it makes.

A traditional statue with a single plume makes a perfect fountain in this formal, lavender-enclosed pool.

Statue fountains

Frequently seen in the gardens of large historic houses, where they form focal points at the end of long vistas or in the centre of garden 'rooms', figurative fountains often feature a maiden or a cherub holding an overflowing urn, or a small boy on a dolphin with water pouring from its mouth. Another choice for a grand garden would be a group of several dolphins or sea horses, each spurting water.

In the days before piped water came to every home, one of the aims of such features was to show off wealth and impress visitors; however, developments in plumbing mean that statue fountains, albeit generally more modest, are now within the scope of any gardener.

Streams

Streams are informal, natural-looking watercourses with a few bends or curves. They are ideal as part of a woodland-style garden, with plants such as ferns and ivies spilling over the banks. A rocky stream also looks good in an alpine garden setting, with low-growing plants blurring the edges.

For a more natural appearance, the width of the stream should vary along its length.

Waterfalls and cascades

A waterfall is often integrated into a natural-looking stream (*see* pages 44–5) or is designed as a way of

A shallow, rock-strewn stream looks completely at home in this informal garden. The vertical marginal planting creates natural height in a flattish site.

bringing water into an informal pond. Achieving a convincing, natural look requires a lot of careful attention to detail but is worth the additional work.

Where two or more formal pools are linked, the water often falls over a flat edge or a jutting lip, giving a minimalist, contemporary look to the feature. Where there is more than one fall, they should be identical to maintain the symmetry and formality. Split-level pools (*see* page 18) are often designed with a modern style of waterfall.

Cascades are really a series of waterfalls. They're usually built to look like a stream running over several rocky outcrops.

Slabs of stone have been used to create this cascade, which tumbles down into a gravel-filled pool.

Don't forget

A pump is usually required to move water, so you will need an electricity supply close by.

Planning and designing

Once you've decided on the type and style of water feature you'd like, you'll need to give some thought to where it will fit into your garden. You may well have your heart set on a certain shape or style of pond, for instance, but it's best to keep your options open until you've measured up and done a few sketches. Inevitably, the site will influence the final outcome. You could easily end up with something quite different from what you first envisaged, simply because it suits the space better.

Choosing the site

Consider the view to the proposed water feature from different parts of the garden. Do you want to be able to see it from the house, to create a focal point, or would you prefer to tuck it away in a secluded corner? And would it look better positioned above ground or at ground level? Before making any decisions, there are various practical requirements to take into account.

Sun, shade and shelter

If you're creating a water feature containing plants, select a site that is in full light for most of the day. For a balanced ecosystem to develop, good plant growth is vital and the

Taking measurements and making drawings will help you to create the perfect water garden.

plants need lots of light. However, if possible avoid a spot that receives full sun at midday, because it causes problems with water evaporation and fish will not be happy.

Keep the water feature away from overhanging trees – leaves will need to be removed regularly to prevent the water becoming foul, and roots can split or lift the liner – but a little shade nearby is pleasant on a hot day, and shelter from wind is necessary to minimize evaporation.

Soil type and drainage

Before settling on a site, it's always worth digging a trial hole to see whether the soil structure is suitable. If the soil is very dry and sandy, you'll need to resite the pond or shore up the hole with sheets of

The whole garden revolves around this pool and its hard landscaping. Meticulous planning, and construction work, has ensured its success.

Pond size

The larger the pond, the more balanced the ecosystem will be, which means the water quality will be better and the pond easier to maintain (*see* page 61). Ideally, a pond will be at least 3 square metres (32 square feet). Remember to include a variety of depths and planting zones (*see* pages 54–7 and 71–91).

A flat site is ideal for a pond. From the grassy bank behind it, to the decking and the pebble beach, this pool has been carefully designed to suit its surroundings.

Design tips

■ Be bold with your ideas. In general, larger ponds are better than small ones. They have the most impact and will also be less work to maintain (see box, opposite).

■ Keep everything simple. Ponds with complicated outlines look too fussy and are difficult to dig and line. In the end, marginal planting will blur the edges anyway.

■ Allow existing garden features to determine the position and shape of your pond. In the case of a formal pond, consider the manmade elements, such as walls of buildings and paths. For an informal pond, echo the forms of the natural elements; the pond needs to look as if it was always in your garden.

■ For a natural effect, make streams as long as possible with wide, sweeping curves, and site them off-centre. Informal waterfalls look best if they are made to follow the contours of the surrounding landscape.

■ If you are designing a formal pond, consider octagons and hexagons as well as squares, circles and rectangles. Alternatively, you can combine straight lines and curves.

■ Formal water features should fit neatly into the hard landscaping and are ideally built using materials that match or complement those used to build your house, or the patio and paths. Similarly, any landscaping materials used for an informal pond should look at home in the surroundings.

■ An informal pond may need some evergreen plants or shrubs with winter interest such as coloured stems around it to ensure it remains appealing all year round.

■ Precision is vital for a formal pond. If you want a rectangular pond to be seen from the patio doors, for example, make sure that it will appear dead centre when you look out onto it. The smallest misalignment will spoil the effect. If it can't be dead centre, place it quite obviously off-centre so it is clear it has been done deliberately.

plywood to support the sides. If it is very waterlogged, the liner could get damaged, so again you'll have to position the pond elsewhere or install a drainage system.

You may need to cater for overflow from a pond in very wet weather, in order to prevent flooding. A bog garden positioned alongside the pond is the most natural way to do this, and it also makes an attractive feature (see pages 42–3). Alternatively, if drainage is really bad, you could install a soakaway drainage system, then make a small indentation in the pond bank directly beside the soakaway to ensure that any excess water will flow into it.

Don't forget

Find out where underground drains and electrical cables run and build the pond well away from them.

Even a simple water feature such as this rill requires a pump and electrical cables – all are hidden from view.

Further considerations

Once you've chosen the site, there are further practicalities to consider. Thinking about these now will give you a good idea of the scale of the project and can save a lot of time and bother later.

Digging and soil removal

A feature that is above ground requires minimal digging, but if you're creating a sunken pond excavation and soil removal will be major considerations.

A small pond can be dug out with a spade and the soil used elsewhere, while larger ponds, long rills and streams are likely to require a mini-digger. Make sure you have access from the road and through the garden. Even small diggers leave a mess, so be prepared to make good other parts of the garden.

Decide on where the soil from the pond will go before you dig. You could consider using excess soil to create banks or other raised features. (*See* also pages 14 and 35–7.)

Water and electricity

If you're using an electric pump in your water feature or are installing a filter system or lighting, you'll need to consider what to do with the cables and water pipes.

You must use armoured cables, which should ideally be fed through protective ducting. It's best to conceal supply pipes in a deep trench running from where they enter the house to the pond (*see* page 33).

Although you can lay the electrical cables yourself, connecting up to the mains supply must always be carried out by a professional. If you need outdoor sockets, they must be fully waterproof and have built-in circuit breakers or safety cut-outs, which cut off the power supply if the cable is damaged by accident.

When it comes to filling and topping up the water feature, you can use either water from the mains or a hosepipe. You might also like to run a hose from a water butt. Rainwater contains fewer nitrates than tap water, which can upset the balance of a natural pond.

Don't forget

It is important to have easy access to your water feature for maintenance and feeding fish, so make sure to allow plenty of room around its sides.

Drawing up a plan

It's always a good idea to make a scale drawing of the garden, or at least the area around the proposed site of the water feature, before you start digging. Include all the existing elements – flower beds, paths and so on. This will give you a bird's eye view of the site, which makes it easier to play around with ideas.

On a separate piece of paper, make some templates of your water feature (again to scale) in different shapes and sizes. Cut these out and try positioning them on your master plan. If it looks good on paper, it will generally look good in reality. Make a list of all the other elements that you want to include, such as a bog garden, a seating area, a walkway and so on, and think about how they're going to fit into your plan.

Safety around the pond

Before you finalize the style and size of your water feature, it is essential to consider safety. Unfortunately, wherever there is water, there is the possibility of drowning, and it can happen in a depth of just a few inches. Although children are at greatest risk, adults can have accidents around water too.

■ Make all surrounding paths and hard landscaping non-slip. Cover wooden decking or railway sleepers with galvanized chicken mesh to give a firm footing all year round.

■ If children are likely to use the garden, surround the water feature with a fence and a locked gate. Fit the pond with a mesh cover, strong enough to support the weight of an adult. Position the mesh on the water's surface so it is not too conspicuous, or put it on a removable frame that fits over the pool edges.

■ Small, raised water features make it harder for children to get to the water, so they're safer than a sunken pond. If you have children of five years old or younger, choose a pebble fountain or a trickle-style water feature (*see* page 48).

Planning checklist

The following questions will prompt you to consider what type of water garden will suit you and your garden and the practicalities involved in creating one. Consider the cost of your preferred option, taking into account labour and equipment hire as well as the construction materials. Be realistic about what you can do yourself within your desired time frame and which aspects are beyond your capabilities and fitness levels. Even if you don't construct the feature yourself, it's important to know what's involved.

Style and design

■ Do you like a tidy-looking, ornamental water feature with neat edges (such as a rill or formal pool) or a more natural effect with lots of surrounding vegetation (for instance a stream or wildlife pond)?

■ Do you feel comfortable with geometric shapes and symmetry or more sinuous, irregular forms? Will the style of water feature you've chosen blend with your garden and look appropriate?

■ If you're creating a formal water feature, will the building materials you're intending to use complement the house?

■ Have you thought about how changes of level, such as a raised pond, a split-level pool or mini-stream with cascades, can provide interest, particularly in a small, flat space?

■ Do you like the idea of sound in the garden, for example the soothing trickle of a pebble fountain or the invigorating gushing of a waterfall?

■ Would you like to include decorative features to add interest, such as stepping stones, bridges and banks? (*See* pages 14–15.)

■ Would you like to light up your water feature at night? (*See* pages 22–3.)

■ Will you want to run pumps for waterfalls and cascades all day long? If not, have you ensured that your design will work without them running?

Considering the practicalities

■ When positioning the water feature, have you considered shelter, shade and sun? Will the plants and wildlife receive adequate amounts of each? (*See* page 24.)

■ If you're planning an informal pond, stream or rill, have you allowed sufficient space for planting around the edge?

■ Do you want to be able to sit beside your water feature? If so, have you considered where you might place the seating? For instance, will you need to install hard surfacing such as decking, paving or gravel?

■ Will you need to install any new paths so you can reach the water feature without stepping on flower beds? And is there enough space around for you to carry out maintenance tasks or feed the fish?

■ Is attracting wildlife important to you? If so, have you built into your pond design the various elements that are attractive to wildlife? (*See* pages 40–1.)

■ Do you know where the utilities, such as the water and sewage pipes, go through the garden, and have you taken these into account in your design?

■ Have you considered how you're going to get water and electricity to the feature and how to hide the pipework? (*See* opposite.)

■ Will the feature be safe, particularly where children are concerned? (*See* opposite.)

■ If you're planning a pond, have you worked out a planting scheme, with plants allocated to their correct depth, for instance submerged, floating, marginal, deep-water and bog plants? (*See* pages 54–7.)

Assessing the workload

■ If you're creating a raised water feature, are you able to build walls yourself, or will you need to hire a brick layer or general builder? ■ If you're making a sunken pond, have you dug a trial hole to see whether the soil is easy to dig? (*See* pages 24–5.)

■ Are you fit enough to excavate the area, or will you need to get someone (or several people) to help you?

■ Will you be able to dig the pond by hand, or will you need a mechanical digger?

■ Will a digger be able to fit into your garden and manoeuvre without causing any damage to surrounding borders and other garden features?

■ Can you drive a digger or will you need to hire a driver?

■ What will you do with the excavated soil? Will there be too much to put on the garden, even if you build banks or other features with the excess, and will you need to arrange to have it removed?

■ Have you considered how you're going to protect the surrounding area if you're shifting soil and moving wheelbarrows around the garden? Perhaps you'll need some planks of wood to avoid compacting the ground, or a large sheet of plywood to protect the lawn?

■ Are you prepared to maintain and clean pumps and filters regularly (often once a week in summer) – particularly for tiny water features – or are you more suited to a more maintenance-free option, such as a wildlife pond? (*See* pages 32–3 and 40–1.)

Equipment and materials

■ Have you researched all the options for buying and hiring tools and equipment, including DIY stores, builders' merchants, local suppliers and aquatic centres?

■ Have you thought through the order of work involved and delivery times of equipment, in order to ensure everything runs smoothly?

■ Have you worked out quantities for materials such as sand and cement correctly and double-checked you've got all your measurements right before ordering?

■ If you need a liner, have you worked out what sort of liner and the size you will need, and ordered it ahead of starting work? (*See* pages 30–1.)

■ Do you want a fountain or other type of water circulation system? If so, do you know how powerful your pump should be? (*See* page 32.)

■ Do you need a filtration system for fish? (*See* pages 33 and 58–9.)

■ If you're planning to hire a digger, have you briefed the contractors in sufficient detail, specifying the position, size and depth of the pond, what you intend to do with the excavated soil, etc?

■ If you have a pump, have you considered all the safety aspects, such as fitting a circuit breaker to protect you from electric shocks and ensuring that power cables are suitable for outdoor use and protected by pipes? (*See* opposite and page 33.)

Making a water garden

Once you've decided what sort of water feature to construct, you'll want the work to go as smoothly as possible. Refer to the checklist on page 27 and gather all the materials you need. Draw up a plan of action, so you know what you want to achieve each day, and bear in mind that most features are easier to construct with two pairs of hands. You can build a water feature any time, but late winter or early spring are generally best for making a pond, as it allows time for the water to settle and warm up before you add the plants.

Tools for construction

Before you start work, check that you have all the relevant tools and make sure they're in good condition. Some items will be useful for almost any style and size of water feature, while others are more specific and required only for certain jobs. For equipment such as liners, pumps and filters, *see* pages 30–3.

Preparing the site

Most of the tools mentioned here are essential for marking out the site and for excavating soil.

Measuring and marking

A tape measure is required for all but tiny water features; it will probably need to be at least 10m (33ft) long. Pegs, stakes, string, a mallet and a builder's square are all useful for creating the shape of a pond. A hosepipe or length of thick rope is helpful for making curvy shapes. Landscaper's spray paint or a plastic bottle filled with sand are useful for marking shapes on the ground.

Moving soil

For ponds, rills, streams and other sunken features, you'll need a spade and a wheelbarrow; even if you're planning to hire a mini-digger, you'll be doing at least some of the work by hand. A fork for loosening compacted ground is also useful, and a shovel is better than a spade for putting loose soil into a wheelbarrow. A trowel and a rake will both come in handy for finer shaping work.

Checking levels

A large spirit level and a wooden plank, or a scaffolding board, will ensure you get your levels right – crucial where water is involved! For a pond, the plank will need to be at least 2m (6ft) long. It will also be useful for accessing the middle of a pond, once it is filled, so you can plant deep-water plants such as water lilies.

Hard landscaping

For building brick walls around raised formal pools and for edging features with pavers and other hard landscaping materials, you'll need a variety of specialist tools.

A bricklayer's trowel is required for working with mortar. Pointing is easier with a raking tool or pointing

When making a pond, the key to success is getting the levels right; use a long spirit level and a plank.

trowel. You'll also need a board for mixing mortar, and a bucket or watering can.

If you're planning to do any woodwork, such as adding decking or making a raised pond out of sleepers, you'll need a saw and screwdrivers. Make sure your saw is sharp, and for larger projects consider buying a jigsaw. You'll also need a drill and drill bits, a claw hammer, nails and screws.

At least some of the digging work will be done by hand. Use a spade or shovel and a wheelbarrow.

A wooden mallet and pegs are useful for marking out the shape of the water feature and checking levels.

Don't forget

You can buy bags of ready-mixed brick-laying mortar and multipurpose concrete from DIY stores to save mixing them yourself.

Creating a bog garden

Bog gardens provide the ideal conditions to grow a range of attractive, lush, colourful plants (*see* pages 82–91). They're particularly suitable for placing alongside informal or wildlife ponds and streams, adding to the natural effect and increasing the range of habitats for creatures that like damp surroundings. However, they also make good stand-alone features. They're usually straightforward to make and once established can be tended as easily as the rest of the garden.

Snakeshead fritillaries and drumstick primulas revel in damp conditions, while the narcissi are in drier ground at the bog's edge.

Bog garden alongside a pond or stream

Apart from looking more natural, one of the main advantages of having a bog garden alongside a water feature is that the water from the pond or stream keeps the soil in the bog garden moist by overflowing and seeping through a permeable membrane.

It's best to include a bog garden in your design when building your water feature, so that you can dig it out at the same time. However, it's simple enough to convert an area beside it afterwards (*see* opposite), so long as hard landscaping isn't in the way. If the water feature is on a slope, choose the lowest side of it for positioning your new boggy area.

A bog garden is constructed in a similar way to a pond, except it is considerably shallower. Also, holes are made in the waterproof liner to allow drainage. This will prevent the area becoming stagnant. Grit is placed on top of the liner to prevent the holes from becoming clogged with soil.

While a special pond liner is needed for a pond, any inexpensive

Bog garden plants are characterized by their abundant foliage. This creates dense ground cover, echoing that found by a natural pond or stream.

How to create a bog garden

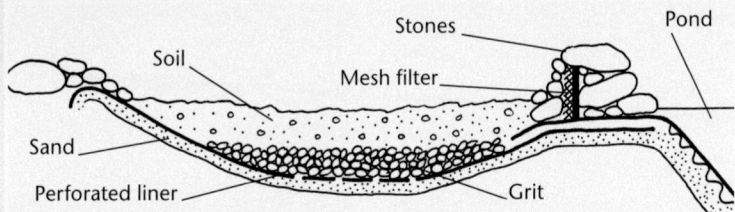

This bog garden has been created alongside an existing pond.

1 Mark out the shape of your bog garden as for a sunken pond (*see* pages 34–5) and empty some of the water out of the pond so you can work on the bog without the pond water flowing into it.

2 Excavate the site of the bog garden to a depth of 30–45cm (12–18in), keeping the topsoil and subsoil separate (*see* pages 35–6). Leave a ridge of soil about 30cm (12in) wide between the pond and bog garden; it should be 2.5–5cm (1–2in) lower than the pond edge.

3 Remove any large stones and other rough material from the base, rake it reasonably smooth, then cover with a layer of sand about 2.5cm (1in) deep.

4 Lay the waterproof liner (polythene or black plastic) on the sand and make drainage holes, spacing them 60–90cm (2–3ft) apart.

5 Tuck the bog garden liner under the pond liner to prevent seepage.

6 Put a 5cm (2in) layer of coarse grit on top of the waterproof liner.

7 Return any subsoil to the hole. Mix plenty of well-rotted compost into the topsoil and shovel it back on top, only partially filling the hole.

8 Build a barrier wall of stones between the pond and bog garden, along the ridge. Place a layer of fine plastic mesh along the back of the barrier wall, on the bog garden side.

9 Finish filling the bog garden with soil, then fill the pond with water to its previous level. Water will seep through the mesh and the rock wall into the bog garden.

10 Trim the liner edges, then add the edging (*see* pages 50–3). Allow the soil to settle for a few days before planting up the bog garden.

waterproof material is acceptable for a bog garden, including polythene sheeting or overlapping black plastic bags. This is because the bog garden liner will be totally covered by soil and there is no contact with sunlight, which can cause damage.

Where the pond and bog garden meet, you must make a ridge wide enough to prevent the bank collapsing into the bog. If you are adding a bog to an existing pond made with a flexible liner, you can simply make an indentation in the pond edge under the liner so excess water flows into the bog.

Bog garden as a stand-alone feature

If you don't have a pond or stream, or haven't got the space to fit a bog garden alongside your water feature, there's nothing to stop you having a bog garden in a separate area of the garden. However, if the bog garden is not located beside a water feature, you'll need to add an irrigation hose or water inlet pipe to ensure the bog garden remains moist and that the soil never dries out. You'll also have to water the bog garden in dry spells. (*See also* box, right.)

Planting and aftercare

Try to avoid walking on the soil of a bog garden. It will be soft to walk on, but more importantly you'll compact it and spoil its structure if you do. Use a plank or stepping stones to get around the garden for planting and maintenance.

Bog plants are planted just like any other garden plants. Dig a hole big enough to take the rootball and place the plant into it, making sure it's at the same depth in the soil as it was in the pot. Backfill around the edges and firm in. Water well.

Feed plants annually with a scattering of blood, fish and bone or other slow-release organic fertilizer.

Adding a thick mulch of fine bark or compost after planting should help to suppress weeds. If your soil is very weedy, it's worth waiting two or three weeks before planting, using this time to remove all new weed growth as it emerges. Thereafter, pull or dig out weeds on a regular basis. If you need to water, weed first since the weeds will be easier to remove from drier soil.

Design tips

■ A bog garden will look more effective if the planting gently merges into the rest of the garden rather than coming to an abrupt end. Include trees or shrubs, and for the outer edges of the bog choose adaptable plants (such as ferns and hardy geraniums) that can cope with both moist and dry conditions.

■ If you can't fit the bog garden beside your pond, try to link the two visually in some way. For example, make a timber walkway between them. Or plant echoing groups of exotic-looking foliage plants, such as bamboo, in both places.

■ Use decking, a bridge or stepping stones (*see* pages 14–15) to link the bog garden with your pond or stream and the rest of the garden.

Making a stream

In essence, an artificial stream consists of a narrow watercourse flowing gently downhill into a pond. The pond at the bottom acts as a reservoir, containing a pump that moves water up via a hidden pipe to the 'source' of the stream and a header pool. A stream can make a lovely natural-looking feature, either as part of a new water garden or added to an existing pond.

Careful use of rocks and plants to hide the liner ensures this stream blends in with its surroundings.

Planning a stream

Plan your stream so it flows slowly down a gradual slope – normally, a gradient of 5cm (2in) per 50cm (20in) is sufficient – or add interest with a waterfall or cascade (*see* page 17). If there is no existing drop and you're making a new pond, you can use the spoil to create a slope. For a realistic effect, and to keep the water flowing well, a stream should meander gently, with no sharp angles. Like a real stream, the width of the bed should vary along its length, but an average of 30cm (12in) works well. Likewise, the depth should vary. Aim for an average of 20cm (8in), using rocks, pebbles or slate chippings on the stream bed to vary the depth.

Wide, deep streams require a huge amount of water to run properly. To reduce the water volume, you can create a series of mini-pools that are deep at the back, shallow at the front and connected by dams and waterfalls, as shown opposite. As well as using less water and looking more interesting than a stream on one level, this design ensures the pools will retain water if the pump is turned off. For a natural look, allow for planting areas (10–15cm/4–6in deep) in the stream bed and marginal zones at intervals along the banks.

Reservoir and header pools

The surface area of the reservoir pond must be at least as much as that of all the rest of the feature. Otherwise, when you start the pump, its water level will drop noticeably. The header (upper) pool can be small – it could just be

Don't forget

A stream will not normally need a filter: if it is well planted and there are no fish present, it should remain clear by itself.

Slate is hardwearing and flat – a perfect choice for a stream. Avoid soft stone, like limestone, which wears away and may alter the chemical balance of the water.

How to make a stream

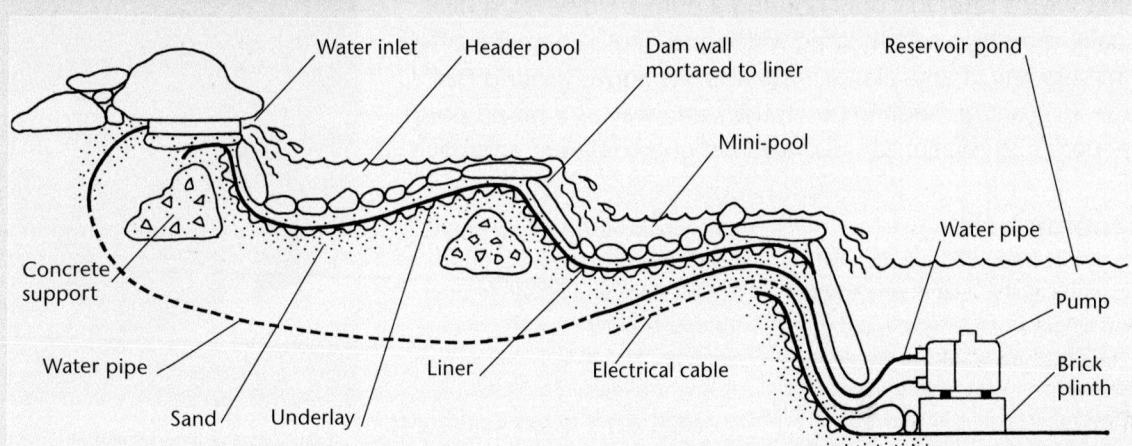

Water inlet · **Header pool** · **Dam wall mortared to liner** · **Reservoir pond** · **Mini-pool** · **Water pipe** · **Concrete support** · **Pump** · **Water pipe** · **Liner** · **Electrical cable** · **Brick plinth** · **Sand** · **Underlay**

This stream has dams making mini-pools and waterfalls. A rigid liner has been used to make the lower (reservoir) pond (for how to make one, *see* page 37).

1 Working up from the reservoir pond, dig out the stream trench making a series of steps. Angle the sides of the trench at about 45 degrees. Make the back of each step more or less vertical and the base drop slightly backwards, to create a mini-pool. Add 5–8cm (2–3in) to the final depth of the stream to allow for sand, underlay and liner. If the ground is at all unstable, make concrete supports under the dams.

2 Dig a straight, parallel trench, about 15–20cm (6–8in) from one side of the stream, to accommodate the water pipe.

3 Line the stream bed (including the mini-pools) with 2.5–5cm (1–2in) of sand. Tamp it down to make a firm base. Add a layer of underlay and then a sheet of flexible liner. Take the excess into the reservoir pond and over the back of the header pool to line the area where the water pipe will lie.

4 Push the liner firmly into the back of each mini-pool, folding the edges neatly, then mortar smooth stones to keep it in place. Where the stream liner meets the edge of the reservoir pond, lay it over the top of the reservoir liner.

5 Build the dam walls with large stones, mortaring the bottom onto the liner. Cover the lip of the step with a flat stone. The rocks at the outside edges of each

dam should be a bit higher than those in the middle of the dam, to prevent water spilling over the sides. Fill all gaps with concrete to ensure the mini-pools are watertight. Place rocks alongside the stream, mortaring where needed to prevent water escaping. Allow at least a week for everything to set fully.

6 Place the pump in the reservoir pond (*see* page 32). Run the water pipe to the header pool via the trench. Mark where it is in case you need access. Use plastic tubing to protect the electrical cable where it exits the pond and the water pipe where it is hidden by stones. Fill the reservoir pond with water. Cover the stream bed and sides with gravel and pebbles of different sizes.

a hollow waterproofed with liner. For a good flow of water, choose a pump that can cope sufficiently with the length of the stream and the volume of water to be moved (*see* page 32).

Don't forget

For a quiet trickle, place the flat stones on the lip flush with the dam wall. For a noisier flow, make them jut slightly out. To funnel the water so as to make a faster flow, you can leave gaps in the top course of the dam rocks.

Marking out the stream

Working up from the reservoir pond (*see* pages 34–7), mark out the stream width about twice that of the finished stream, allowing for wide bends. Mark the position of any dams, mini-pools and planting bays. Check levels (*see* pages 34–5).

Allow for installing an electricity supply to run the pump. This must be safe and hidden (*see* page 33).

See pages 54–5 for ideas on planting in and around the stream.

You may also want to add stepping stones or a simple wooden bridge (*see* pages 14–15).

Liners

Stream beds are best made with a single sheet of flexible liner, but preformed sections are available for use in combination with sheet liners. If using flexible liner and underlay, allow for any bends in the stream when calculating their width, and add 45cm (18in) to their length to allow for a reasonable overlap at both ends.

There is something very pleasing about glimpsing colourful flashes of gold, white and red as ornamental fish swim among water lily pads. Many people build ponds just so they can keep fish and it can become an absorbing hobby. Fish are particularly suitable for formal ponds, but they can be put into almost any water feature, so long as a few rules about space and water quality are observed.

Fish need some shade. Water lily leaves are ideal for providing this.

Creating a suitable environment

If you're keeping fish, you need a pond that is at least 60cm (24in) deep. Up to two thirds of the water's surface must be shaded to prevent it warming up too much in hot weather. Water lilies and other aquatics with floating leaves will do the trick. These also provide places for the fish to hide from predators.

If you have just built your pond, wait about four weeks, until the plants have had time to establish, before introducing fish. The water also needs time to settle and – if you have filled the pond from a tap – allow chemicals to break down. Ideally, add fish in late spring or early summer, when the water is around 10°C (50°F).

Most fish like to feed on the bottom of a pond, churning up the silt and disturbing plants. It's wise to use planting baskets if you keep fish.

The water in a fish pond

A pond dedicated to fish will usually need a biological filter to keep the water clean. The only exception to this would be an extremely large pond, very lightly stocked with fish, which live naturally and find their own food. All fish ponds should also have a pump or fountain to circulate and aerate the water. (See also pages 32–3.)

Check water quality regularly, as problems with this will affect fish health. Partial water changes on a regular basis will help ensure good quality. In low-rainfall areas, you will need to top up regularly anyway.

(See also pages 32–3.)

Don't forget

Add a dechlorinator to any tap water that you add to the pond, to remove chlorine and other disinfectants that could harm the fish.

As goldfish like to spend time at the surface, they can easily be watched at close quarters.

Buying and releasing fish

Buy fish from a respected supplier. Choose those at least 8cm (3in) long, as these will adapt more easily to a new environment than smaller ones. Pick active fish with clean, healthy scales, no marks or blemishes, clear eyes and erect fins with neat edges. If one looks unwell (see Fish health, opposite), don't buy others in the same tank.

The fish you buy should be packed in polythene bags full of water and some air. Put the bag in a cool, dark place for the journey home. Float the bag in the pond in a shady spot for 20–30 minutes before releasing the fish to give them time to adjust to the new temperature.

Equipment

For a fish pond, a pump or fountain to circulate water is vital. A biological filter will also be required in most cases, to keep the water clean, and a UV filter as well if you want the water to be crystal clear. Bear this in mind when you are planning your pond, as pumps require an electrical supply. Similarly, biological filters and UV filters are positioned outside the pond and drain back into it, so you'll need to think about where to site them and how to hide them. In icy weather, it is essential that a fish pond doesn't freeze. An electric pond heater will keep a permanent hole in the ice; put it in the pond when frost is forecast. (See also page 65, Preventative measures.)

Then gently allow some pond water into the bag and allow them to swim out. Introduce fish a few at a time, over a period of months.

Feeding fish

In larger ponds, fish will find their own food, including tadpoles, midges and mosquitoes. However, most fish ponds are far too heavily stocked for the fish to find enough natural food by themselves, so you should also feed them with a balanced fish food to ensure they are getting all the nutrients they need. Do not feed when the water is under 5°C (41°F). Never overfeed, as food left in the water will increase problems such as algae; remove any food not consumed after five minutes.

Fish varieties

The most popular fish are goldfish and their highly bred relatives, which include shubunkins and comets.

GOLDFISH – Come in a range of colours including orange, yellow, cream and spotted. They live for around 20 years and grow to around 30cm (12in).

SHUBUNKINS – Basically, these are goldfish with some transparent scales. Their colours include white, yellow, red, blue and black. The Bristol shubunkin has a larger tail fin.

COMETS – Like goldfish, except with bigger fins all round and their tail fins are deeply forked. The Sarasa comet is red and white.

ORFE – Either gold or blue, these grow up to 45cm (18in) long and need well-aerated water, so are suitable only for larger ponds.

How many fish?

Although you will want at least four or five fish for effect, do not overstock because overcrowding encourages water-quality problems. Remember too that fish grow and when happy may breed. As a guide, if your pond has a biological filter, allow around 2.5cm (1in) of fish per 40 litres (10 gallons) of water.

These fish are all suitable for garden ponds.
① Orfe.
② Shubunkin.
③ Sarasa comet.

Fish health

If the water quality is good and the pond well cared for, fish can resist most ailments, but problems can be introduced with new fish. Ideally, quarantine new fish in a separate pond or aquarium for two weeks before introducing them to an established pond where fish are already present. Try to buy all your fish from the same source if possible.

Symptoms of poor health include lethargy, rapid breathing, a slimy-looking skin, red streaks or patches, ulcers, damaged scales, and ragged or clamped fins. White spots and fluffy growths may indicate parasitic or fungal diseases. Fish can also suffer from larger parasites like lice or flukes, which make them 'scratch' themselves on objects and may be visible on the scales.

If you spot a sick fish, first check that there is no problem with the water quality and that all the equipment is functioning as it should. If only one fish is affected, it may be easier to remove it to an aquarium for treatment, but in many cases the whole pond will need to be treated and any underlying problem fixed. Consult a specialist retailer or vet for advice if necessary.

Herons

Once a heron has found a pond stocked with fish, it may become a regular visitor. As herons normally land on ground near to, rather than on, a pond, a sturdy netting fence, 45–60cm (18–24in) high, around the pond should be enough of a deterrent. If not, you might need to put a net over the pond as well. Tall marginal plants also help to make access difficult.

Koi carp

Koi carp are specialist fish that need deep water – a minimum of around 1.2–1.5m (4–5ft), lots of space and special koi food. They grow very large and like to eat pond plants, so are not suitable for the average garden pond. Pump or gravity-fed koi filters require complex pipework. Ask for advice at an aquatic centre.

Maintaining a water garden

The amount of maintenance needed for a water feature depends on its size and type. If you have a tiny feature without plants, you will need to clean the insides and change the water regularly. With a natural pond, the tricky part tends to be getting conditions right at the start but, once a good ecosystem is established, it is more or less self-sustaining. Most pond plants thrive with little attention, though some will need to be kept in check. An ornamental fish pond needs a bit more work.

A healthy pond

In mid- or late summer, and within two or three months of adding the plants, most new ponds should have clear water, and plenty of aquatic creatures will have taken up residence. These are good indicators of a healthy pond and subsequent pond troubles should be minimal, but *see* pages 66–7 if you have have any concerns or if problems do crop up.

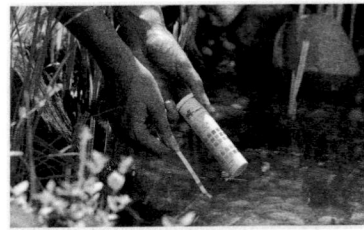

If you are worried about your pond water, it's worth doing a test using a simple kit from any aquatic centre.

Natural ponds

When you first fill a pond, the water inevitably turns green. It looks bad, but it really won't be long before the murkiness disappears. Algae thrive in the nitrate-rich tap water used to fill a pond, but as plants and creatures start to compete for nutrients, the algae starve or are eaten. Once the plants are growing well and myriad tiny creatures have arrived, the nutrients (that is, decomposing plant material and dead creatures) and the consumers of nutrients (living plants and creatures) quickly balance out and water quality improves.

Similarly, an established pond will go murky every spring as the water warms up and the algae have a growth spurt. But if you have the right types of plant in the right numbers (*see* pages 54–5), the ecosystem soon balances out again and the water suddenly clears.

Ornamental ponds

Water problems are more likely in a pond where a natural biological balance is not possible because there is not a sufficient variety or number of plants to attract wildlife. For example, formal, ornamental ponds tend to have minimal planting and very often contain fish, which will prey on any beneficial creatures.

Keeping the water in an ornamental pond clear and well oxygenated – and this is crucial if you have fish – almost certainly means investing in technology and running a pump and a filter (*see* pages 32–3 and 58–9).

Water quality

If you stock fish, it's wise to test the water regularly. Most pond fish like a pH (acidity/alkalinity) level between 7 and 8, and low or zero levels of waste products like nitrates or ammonia. If you do not have fish, water testing can tell you if your pond would benefit from water changes to reduce algae, or if the pH is not right for certain plants. Test kits check pH, hardness and nutrients such as nitrates. (*See also* page 67.)

Top tips

There are a few things that you can do to help Mother Nature.

■ Use rainwater to top up if possible. If using tap water, use a dechlorinator.

■ Ensure that around half of the water's surface is still open to the sky and floating plants are shading other areas.

■ As any nearby trees and shrubs grow, ensure the pond still has plenty of sun and there are no overhanging branches that will drop leaves into the water.

A pond like this, with a balance of deep-water, surface and marginal plants kept under control, and a variety of water creatures living in it, will stay healthy.

Pond repairs and renovation

As ponds and other water features begin to age, they can develop problems with their structure. Hard winters with lots of very icy weather are particularly troublesome, but sometimes difficulties occur simply because the pond was not constructed properly in the first place. Before you condemn your water feature, it's worth investigating whether it can be repaired or renovated. Often a little tender loving care is all that is needed.

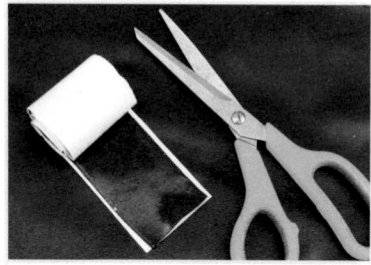

Various products are available online or in aquatic centres for repairing punctures or leaks in a flexible liner.

Fixing a flexible liner

Cheap flexible liners wear out after a few years, so repairs are not really possible or worthwhile, but butyl and epalyn can be fixed with repair kits that are readily available from pond suppliers. Repair small holes with mastic tape or repair strips, and cover larger ones with an offcut of butyl or epalyn stuck down with waterproof adhesive.

Repairing the hole

If necessary, empty the pond to the site of the leak – the water may already have dropped to this level. Clean the liner's surface well with solvent to remove dirt and algae. Feel the site of the leak to see if there is anything sharp poking through. If there isn't, use a repair strip or an offcut of liner and a suitable adhesive, following the instructions

to ensure the two surfaces stick together firmly before you start to refill the pond.

Removing sharp objects

If the hole has been caused by a sharp object that has worked its way through the soil, make the hole slightly larger and either try to remove the culprit or slip a piece of pond underlay through the hole to cushion it. Otherwise, you will have to work from the top of the pond, removing any edging and peeling back the liner to the site of the hole,

Emptying and cleaning a pond is a messy job. Choose a dry day, wear old clothes, and be careful not to cause any further damage to the liner.

Emptying the pond

Move the plants to a shady spot, taking the chance to divide and thin if needed. Put deep-water, oxygenating and floating plants in buckets of pond water; stand marginals in trays of water. Catch fish or frogs in a net and put them in the buckets. The rest of the water can go on flower beds, but look out for tiny creatures and add them to the buckets.

Scoop up the silt, reserving some to go back into the pond to help creatures settle back in. Compost the rest of the mud. Scrub and hose down the liner.

Half fill the pond (if you use tap water, add a dechlorinator to neutralize the disinfectants), then replace the deep-water, oxygenating and floating plants. Add the reserved silt. Finish filling the pond and replace the marginals.

Renovating an overgrown pond

If you inherit a pond that is badly overgrown or looking the worse for wear, it's often worth giving it a facelift, especially if the pond structure is sound and any surrounding hard landscaping is still in good condition.

A fork or rake is useful for removing any plant material you can reach from the bank.

■ Just removing the build-up of algae and weeds will instantly make the pond look better.

■ Clearing overgrown marginals and other plants is best tackled bit by bit over several years so as not to destroy the existing habitat (you might not like it, but there will be plenty of small creatures that do). Aim to remove about a third of overgrowth each year. Leave sections of the pond undisturbed, especially at the margins, and do the work in autumn to help wildlife survive the disruption.

■ You may have to use secateurs and small pruning saws to remove some of the larger plants: be careful not to damage the liner.

■ Where there is a build-up of silt and debris on the pond floor, remove as much of this as necessary, scooping it into a bucket or plastic trug, but do leave some for creatures to hide in. Pile up what you've removed in a shady spot at the side of the pond for about 24 hours, so any creatures you've inadvertently taken out can climb back in. Silt removal will stir up the pond water, which will take a day or two to resettle.

then either removing the sharp object or padding it with underlay. This is a risky job, because the liner may not go back into place easily or you might create other holes, but it's worth trying when the alternative is to replace the liner completely.

Mending a rigid liner

A rigid liner is likely to crack where the ground underneath has settled, reducing its support and putting the liner under pressure from the weight of the water. Cracks may also appear around the lip. If it is a fibreglass liner, you can fix small holes with fibreglass patches and epoxy adhesive, but long cracks caused by lack of support will continue to form. In most cases, once a rigid liner has started to leak, it is best to empty the pond and replace it.

Repairing cracked concrete

Ponds and rills constructed with concrete are particularly vulnerable to cracking during icy weather (*see* right for preventative measures). There are two main solutions: repair the cracks or remove everything from the pond, clean it and then line it with pond underlay and flexible liner (*see* pages 30 and 36).

To repair hairline cracks, clean the surface, then paint the area with two or three coats of waterproof sealant. With larger cracks, chip out the crack using a cold chisel and club hammer, making it deeper and wider. Remove any loose material, then fill the hole with good-quality waterproof mastic. Cover this with waterproofing sealant or waterproof paint. (*See also* page 31.)

Preventative measures

Extremes of weather can cause damage. A flexible liner exposed to strong sunshine is liable to crack; check regularly that all edges are hidden. Ice puts pressure on a pond's walls; float an empty plastic bottle or ball on top of the water, before it freezes, to absorb some of the expansion.

Pond problems and remedies

If you've built your pond carefully and achieved a reasonable balance between the plants, water and aquatic life (*see* page 61), there is not much that can go wrong. As with any other part of the garden, ponds can have pests, diseases and weeds, but few of these cause serious problems and most can be kept under control with prompt action and regular maintenance (*see* pages 68–9).

Plant pests

There are a few pond dwellers that could become pests in sufficient numbers, but will usually be eaten by fish and other aquatic life before this happens.

Caddisfly larvae

These make themselves a protective home by covering their body with grit, sand and pieces of plant that they find in the pond. They attack buds, stems and roots.
Prevention and control A healthy, established pond will contain plenty of other creatures that keep numbers under control.

China mark caterpillar

The brown-and-white china mark moth lays its eggs on the floating leaves of pond plants, including water lilies and duckweed. When the caterpillars hatch out they cut holes in the leaves, using the pieces to make cocoons on the leaf undersides.
Prevention and control The damage is only cosmetic. Pick the cocoons off precious ornamentals.

Chironomid midges

The larvae of these non-biting midges eat the edges of floating leaves and plant roots. Some are called bloodworms and are red, while others are transparent and hardly visible. The midges have long, slender bodies and long legs.
Prevention and control New ponds may suffer from some damage but, as the pond establishes, the other inhabitants will start to keep the larvae numbers down.

False leaf-mining midge

These midges, like the similar leaf-mining midges, produce larvae that tend not to tunnel like other leaf miners, but instead nibble away at the edges of water lily leaves, eating into the soft tissue until all that's left is a skeleton of veins.
Prevention and control Small water lilies in tubs or tiny ponds seem to be most at risk. New ponds may suffer initially until a balanced ecosystem is established. Regularly hose the leaves with water to keep the larvae at bay. With bad infestations, remove and destroy all the leaves. The new growth should be free from the pest.

Water lily aphid

This aphid disfigures leaves and flower buds and is accompanied by black sooty mould, which grows on the aphid excrement (honeydew).
Prevention and control Hose the floating foliage with a jet of water to wash the aphids into the pond.

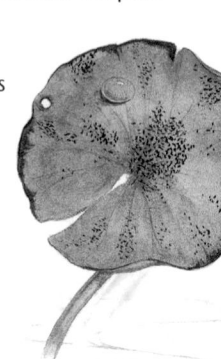

Water lily beetle

The yellow-brown water lily beetle makes long, narrow, wiggly holes in water lily leaves from late spring, and their larvae do similar damage from midsummer. Flowers may also be eaten.
Prevention and control Where you can reach the leaves, pick off the beetles and larvae. Remove badly damaged leaves, because these will rot and upset the water balance.

Plant diseases

Diseases are rare among water plants, and it is mainly water lilies that are likely to succumb to crown rot and leaf spot.

Water lily crown rot

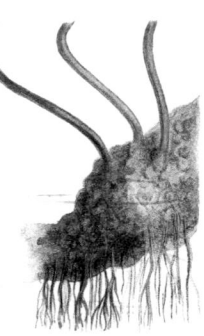

This fungal disease affects flowering and attacks the leaves, which turn yellow and drop off the plant. It spreads very quickly, soon infecting the crown and roots.

Prevention and control Lift affected plants, wash off the soil and cut out any rotting or diseased parts of the crown. Replant the remaining pieces but keep them in a tub of water for a few weeks to ensure they are disease-free before returning them to the pond.

Leaf spot

Various plants, including water lilies, rhizomatous irises (*see* right) and primulas in damp soil, develop concentric red or grey-brown spots on the upper and lower surfaces of the leaves, which eventually rot. It is disfiguring but not serious.

Prevention and control In all cases, remove affected leaves as soon as you see the spots.

Pond weeds

Algae and duckweed are unsightly and can quickly cover the surface of ponds.

ALGAE

This is by far the most common problem in ponds. It mainly occurs as blanketweed, which forms sheets of soft, silky green strands that spread rapidly through the water. Scummy, clotted algal growths like curdled milk are also common; these disperse when touched.

Remove blanketweed with a rake or net, or by twisting it round a cane (*see* page 68). Add more floating plants to shade the water and keep it cooler. Remove some of the silt from the pond each year (*see* page 65). Barley straw logs, available from aquatic centres, may help; put them into the pond in late winter so they break down before the water warms up. Replace every four months. There are also chemical treatments.

DUCKWEED

This tiny, bright green floating plant often arrives with other aquatic plant or pond life. It can spread very rapidly, covering the water's surface and getting into other plants. Check all new plants before putting them into the water. It is worth quarantining them in a tub of water for a couple of weeks to ensure they do not harbour duckweed.

You can easily control duckweed just by fishing it out with a net on a weekly basis. There are also bacterial controls, said to be harmless to other pond life.

Testing the water

If you want fish, before adding them and regularly through the year, check ammonia, nitrite, nitrate and pH levels (*see also* page 61). If the fish look unwell (*see* page 59), do a full water test. As well as filters (*see* page 33), there are various products to improve and alter water quality for fish.

Water testing is not so vital if you do not have fish. However, if the water is always cloudy, plants are not thriving and pond creatures are few or absent, it is worth doing. Causes of poor water quality include excessive silt, which should be removed, too few or too many plants (*see* pages 54–5) or frequent topping up with chlorinated tap water. Try a partial water change of about 25 per cent, using rainwater if possible. If you are still having problems, seek advice from an aquatic centre.

Predators

In a fishpond, these creatures can be pests. Elsewhere, they may be regarded as part of the natural food chain and can safely be left alone and even encouraged.

DRAGONFLY LARVAE Dragonfly larvae (or nymphs) devour anything that they can find, small fish and tadpoles included. Once they have flown away as adults, they eat all kinds of flying insects, including mosquitoes and midges. Damselfy larvae are less voracious than dragonfly larvae.

GREAT DIVING BEETLE This is a vicious beetle (its larvae even more so), preying on small fish, tadpoles and newts. The larvae look like slim dragonfly nymphs but with claws on their heads. If you want to remove them, try catching them with a net.

WHIRLIGIG BEETLE These entertaining little creatures (barely 6mm/¼in long but with two pairs of eyes) swim around in gangs, mostly eating other pond insects but also attacking small fry. If this worries you, remove them with a net.

WATER BOATMAN It may be only 1.5cm (½in) long, but the water boatman (*see also* page 41), also known as the backswimmer, catches and kills tadpoles, small fish, even great diving beetle larvae, with a toxic bite. If you want to, try catching them in a net.

Choosing water lilies

In the world of water plants, water lilies are the star attraction – the chorus and variety act all rolled into one. They have no near rivals when it comes to beauty, flower colour, size range and performance. However, most ponds or pools can support only one or two such prima donnas, so you must resist temptation and limit your choice. It's far better to have one flourishing plant than several struggling ones.

Water lilies have rounded to slightly pointed leaves with a deep notch in one side. The long stem attaches in the middle of the leaf, which floats on the water's surface. The flowers are cup- to star-shaped, with slender, slightly incurved petals. They are suitable for all types of pond except the very natural, but are most fitting in formal and semi-formal ponds.

Water lilies can be roughly divided into four groups according to eventual spread, although there is some overlap between adjacent groups. The overall size of the water lily tends to determine the size of the flowers.

MINIATURE (dwarf, pygmy)
PD 10–30cm (4–12in), S 60cm (24in)
SMALL
PD 15–45cm (6–18in), S to 1.2m (4ft)
MEDIUM
PD 30–60cm (12–24in), S to 1.5m (5ft)
LARGE
PD 45–90cm (1½–3ft), S to 2.5m (8ft)

Growing water lilies

Choose water lilies that will be happy with the size and depth of your pond. In shallow or cramped conditions, leaves will be small and

The fragrant *Nymphaea* 'Rose Arey'

there will be few flowers. The plants relish sun and still water. They will survive in a pond with a fountain, but put them as far from it as possible and don't run it continuously.

Plant them in containers of loamy soil, lowering them gradually into the pond (*see* pages 56–7). Feed annually with special water lily fertilizer (*see* page 68). Divide every three or four years (*see* pages 62–3).

GOOD WATER LILIES

Nymphaea 'Aurora' – Miniature; yellow-red flowers, becoming darker with age.

N. 'Charles de Meurville' – Large; dark pink-red centre petals, paler outer ones.

N. 'Fire Crest' – Small to medium; rich-pink flowers with orange stamens.

N. 'Gonnère' – Medium; yellow-centred, white, many-petalled, double flowers.

N. 'Joey Tomocik' – Large; clear-yellow flowers.

N. 'Marliacea Chromatella' – Medium to large; yellow flowers.

N. 'Paul Hariot' – Miniature to small; creamy-orange flowers fading to pink.

N. 'Perry's Baby Red' – Small; deep-red double flowers.

N. 'Rose Arey' (*see* above) – Medium; scented, rose-pink flowers.

N. 'Virginalis' – Medium; white fragrant flowers.

Nymphoides peltata
Floating heart, Water fringe
○ e⁺ ❖ SUMMER
PD 15–60cm (6–24in), S 2m (6ft) or more

Little yellow, star-shaped flowers pop up between the leaves of this fast-spreading water plant all through summer. The leaves are like those of a water lily but smaller. Its rapid growth means it needs regular hacking back to prevent it from taking over, but does make it useful for providing cover in new ponds while other plants are establishing. Division: summer.

Orontium aquaticum Golden club
○ ❖ LATE SPRING to MIDSUMMER
PD 15–45cm (6–18in), S 60–75cm (24–30in)

With flowerheads like little fingers pointing skywards and upright, narrow, blue-green leaves, this is an attractive plant for any pond. The tips of the white flowerheads are covered in tiny yellow flowers. The leaves tend to cluster upright at the surface, which gives the plant a slightly crowded appearance, but it makes a good contrast with spreading plants that float on the water's surface such as water lilies. Division: spring.

Floating plants

There are a few plants that float on the surface of the water and do not require any soil to grow. Invaluable for the shade they cast over the water, which reduces algal growth, they are also attractive and intriguing. As they spread over the water's surface, they provide habitat and hiding places for tadpoles and other pond creatures. Most are small individually but increase rapidly and can spread very widely. Thin plants as necessary (*see* page 62).

Hydrocharis morsus-ranae
Frogbit
○ pH↑ e⁺ ❖ SUMMER
H 2.5–5cm (1–2in), S 0.5–1m (20–40in)

With pretty, three-petalled white flowers and leaves rather like those of a minute water lily, this is a lovely plant for ponds of any size. It is slow to spread and overwinters as dormant buds on the pond bottom; fish some of these out and keep them in a jam jar or tray of wet mud under cover to make sure you maintain your stock of plants.

Lemna trisulca
Ivy-leaved duckweed
○ ◑ e⁺ ❖ SPRING to AUTUMN
H just below the surface of the water
S 1.5m (5ft) or less

This is the only duckweed that can be allowed to spread. Its tiny, star-shaped clusters of frond-like leaves float just below the surface of the water, each with a root or two. It needs no special attention; simply thin it out if it gets too dense. The plants overwinter at the bottom of the pond. It is ideal for a natural rather than formal pond.

Stratiotes aloides Water soldier
○ ◑ pH↑ e⁺ ❖ MIDSUMMER
H to 10cm (4in), S 0.5–1m (20–40in)

Water soldier spends much of its time just below the surface, emerging to flower in midsummer. It forms starbursts of sword-shaped leaves and bears three-petalled white flowers, 3cm (1¼in) across. After flowering the plant sinks, overwintering as dormant buds on the pond bottom. It needs at least 30cm (12in) of water. It multiplies fast; as new soldiers appear, remove older ones.

Trapa natans Water chestnut
○ ✿ ❖ SUMMER
H 2.5cm (1in), S 1m (40in)

Although the white flowers and nut-like fruits are rarely seen in our climate, this is worth growing for its attractive leaves. They are diamond-shaped with serrated edges and sometimes dark mottling. The leaf-stalks are swollen, making the plant buoyant. Float it on the surface or grow it in a basket. It may suffer badly in poor summers and is killed by frost, so overwinter it in trays or jars of pond water in a frost-free place.

Utricularia vulgaris Common bladderwort, Greater bladderwort
○ pH↓ e⁺ ❖ SUMMER
H 20cm (8in), S 1m (40in)

The fine filigree foliage of this sprawling bladderwort has air-capturing bristles that enable it to float just under the surface. In summer pretty yellow flowers emerge on dark stems. The plant lives on tiny insect larvae, which it captures in bladders attached to the leaves. In winter it dies down to dormant buds, but it will reappear in spring.

Oxygenators

Oxygenators are submerged below the surface of the water. They are grown for their ability to keep pond water healthy, by absorbing carbon dioxide through their leaves, which discourages algae. They also provide pond dwellers with food and a place to deposit eggs. Most are small, individual plants but multiply to make large clumps. Oxygenators are sold as bunches tied with a weight. If the pond has soil at the bottom, drop them in and they will sink and take root. Otherwise, plant them in containers. When these plants start to lose their vigour, or you need to have a supply in reserve, it's easy to grow replacements (*see* page 62). For the best ecosystem, use native plants (*see* Key, page 71). The spreads given here are an estimated size after one growing season.

Callitriche hermaphroditica
Autumn starwort
○ ◐ e⁺ ❖ SUMMER
PD 5–60cm (2–24in), **S** 50cm (20in) or more

This evergreen plant flourishes near the bottom of the pond. It has narrow, pale green leaves on slender stems and tiny flowers in summer. To keep it in check, plant it in a container. As colonies may die off over the winter, cut off and replant some vigorous stems in spring or summer for a continued supply.

Ceratophyllum demersum
Hornwort
○ ◐ e⁺ ❖ SUMMER
PD 60–90cm (24–36in), **S** 30–60cm (12–24in)

This hornwort is grown mainly for its delicate whorls of dark green leaves. Its stems have virtually no roots and in summer float in the water. Tiny flowers appear in summer – males are white, females green. The plant overwinters as small dormant buds in the bottom of the pond. Grow fresh plants by breaking off pieces of stem and dropping them back in the water in spring or summer.

Eleocharis acicularis Hairgrass
○ ◐ e⁺ ❖ SUMMER to AUTUMN
PD 10–30cm (4–12in), **S** indefinite

This small sedge looks very similar to grass, and when happy spreads over the bottom of a pond like turf. The 'leaves' are actually flowering stems; if the plant is grown as a marginal, they bear tiny white flowers from scaly brown buds. It deserves to be grown more widely in outdoor ponds because it makes a useful oxygenator. To make more plants, break up the mats of turf in spring or summer.

Elodea canadensis
Canadian pondweed
○ ◐ ❖ SPRING to AUTUMN
PD 10–60cm (4–24in), **S** 2m (6ft) or more

One of the most common and most prolific oxygenators, Canadian pondweed is best where it can easily be kept under control by regular cutting back and removal. It has branching stems covered with whorls of narrow, curly leaves and floating purplish flowers on fine, long stems in summer. Plant it in containers or allow it to float freely. Because of its invasive nature, never put it into the wild.

Fontinalis antipyretica Willow moss
○ ◐ e⁺ ❖ YEAR-ROUND
PD 10–60cm (4–24in), **S** to 25cm (10in)

This slow-growing, evergreen, water-loving moss has dark green oval leaves that overlap each other like scales. They are produced on slender stems with many branches. It prefers moving water, but tolerates still ponds. Plant it in clumps in shallowish water. To make new plants, divide in spring or summer.

Hippuris vulgaris Mare's-tail
○ e⁺ ❖ SUMMER
PD 10–30cm (4–12in), **S** indefinite

This oxygenator has tall, unbranched dark stems clothed in whorls of narrow green leaves. They grow under water and, in summer, emerge above the surface, making an eye-catching and unusual display and meaning the plant can also be grown as a marginal plant at the pond's edge. Like most oxygenators, it can spread rapidly, so it is best planted in a container and allowed to form attractive, but controlled clumps.

Myriophyllum spicatum
Spiked water milfoil
○ pH↑ e⁺ ❖ SUMMER
PD 30–60cm (12–24in), **S** indefinite

The bronze-green or bright green leaves of this oxygenator are feathery and delicate-looking, making it an attractive addition to the watery depths of the pond. In summer, tiny orange- or yellow-red flowers appear in spikes just above the water's surface. It is fast-growing, so it is good for helping to establish a new pond.

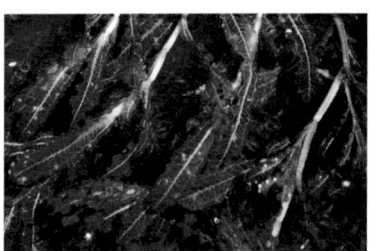

Potamogeton crispus
Curled pondweed
○ ◑ e⁺ ❖ SUMMER
PD and **S** to 1.5m (5ft)

Curled pondweed differs from most oxygenators in that its wavy-edged, long, leathery dark green leaves are comparatively large. In strong light they have a red tinge. Tiny pink-white flowers are borne above the surface of the water. In a muddy pond it will spread quickly, so plant it in a container if you want to keep it in check. It is also happy as a marginal plant.

Hottonia palustris Water violet
○ pH↓ e⁺ ❖ SPRING
PD 10–30cm (4–12in), **S** 30–90cm (12–36in)

Water violet likes clear water in a well-established pool, doing best when planted into mud at the bottom or in a container. In spring, spikes above the water's surface bear pale pink flowers with yellow throats, like small primroses. It has finely divided, pale green leaves that produce wide rosettes at the ends of the stems. It dies down to dormant buds in winter; to be sure of a continued supply of plants, divide clumps in spring.

Myriophyllum verticillatum
Whorled water milfoil
○ pH↑ e⁺ ❖ SUMMER
PD 30–60cm (12–24in), **S** 1m (40in)

Plant this milfoil in a container and place it in deep water, where its long stems clothed in whorls of feathery, bright green leaves can float up towards the surface. In summer its tiny yellow flowers are carried in spikes about 15cm (6in) tall just above the water's surface. The plant overwinters as dormant buds, but it is wise to start new plants in spring or summer to maintain your supply.

Ranunculus aquatilis
Water crowfoot
○ ◑ e⁺ ❖ EARLY SUMMER
PD 15–60cm (6–24in), **S** 10–50cm (4–20in)

This evergreen buttercup relative is grown for its flowers as well as its cleansing abilities. It has feathery leaves below the water and clover-like ones floating on top. In early summer the floating leaves are topped by white, yellow-centred flowers. Grow it in a submerged container or in the pond margins. It is short-lived, so divide in spring or autumn to make new plants.

Marginal plants

Marginal plants grow in the shallows around the edge of a pond, softening the edges and helping it blend in with its surroundings. They include a variety of shapes, sizes and colours; some have eye-catching flowers, while others are grown mainly for their foliage. Most like to have their feet in water and tolerate continuously damp soil. The majority have the potential to outgrow their allocated space. These plants need lifting and dividing regularly (*see* pages 62–3) to keep them under control (an indication is given in the plant descriptions of the best time of year to do this).

Acorus calamus 'Variegatus'
Sweet flag
○ ❖ MIDSUMMER

H to 90cm (3ft), **S** 60cm (24in)

Growing most happily in water about 23cm (9in) deep or shallower, this plant with iris-like leaves has creamy-white and green stripes on its foliage. The leaves, which can be up to 1.5m (5ft) long, are arranged in a fan and smell of tangerines when crushed. The flowers stick out from the leaves like small spikes and are not particularly decorative. Division: spring.

Acorus gramineus Japanese rush
○ ❖ MIDSUMMER

H 8–35cm (3–14in), **S** 10–15cm (4–6in)

More grassy than sweet flag (*see* left), the Japanese rush makes a mop-head of lax leaves. There are two outstanding variegated varieties: 'Ogon' (shown above) has pale green and cream stripes, while those of 'Variegatus' are yellow and cream. Both rarely exceed 25cm (10in) in height. Grow all these rushes in water about 10cm (4in) deep. They look especially good in formal and semi-formal ponds. Division: spring.

Alisma plantago-aquatica
Water plantain
○ e⁺ ❖ MID- to LATE SUMMER

H to 75cm (30in), **S** 45cm (18in)

Although it flowers most profusely in water 15cm (6in) deep, this marginal can be grown up to 30cm (12in) deep. Ideal for a large informal pond, it has airy sprays of tiny white or pale pink flowers and oval green leaves. After flowering, remove the flower stems to avoid prolific self-seeding. Division: late spring.

Butomus umbellatus
Flowering rush
○ e⁺ ❖ LATE SUMMER

H to 1.5m (5ft), **S** 45–60cm (18–24in)

This marginal plant likes to have its feet in rich mud, but will tolerate water to 25cm (10in) deep. Its clumps of narrow, twisted, grass-like leaves make a good hiding place for small pond dwellers. The tall, straight flower stem carries a head of pink, scented flowers, making a great display in late summer, particularly in an informal or wildlife pond. Selected forms with dark pink or white flowers are also available. Division: early spring.

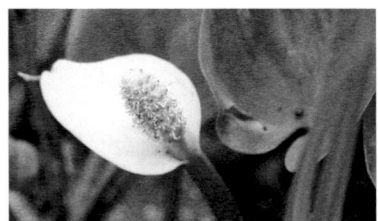

Calla palustris Bog arum
○ ❖ MIDSUMMER

H 25cm (10in), **S** 60cm (24in)

Bog arum has large, heart-shaped, glossy dark green (often semi-evergreen) leaves growing in a dense, upright clump. The flowers consist of a white spathe surrounding a spike of tiny flowers, which develop into red berries in autumn. Bog arum is happiest in water up to 8cm (3in) deep, where it soon spreads to form a good-sized clump. Division: spring.

Caltha palustris
Kingcup, Marsh marigold
○ e⁺ ❖ SPRING to EARLY SUMMER
H to 40cm (16in), **S** 45cm (18in)

Our native kingcup is valuable for its early flowers, which resemble very large buttercups, equally bright yellow and glossy. It has rounded, kidney-shaped leaves. Although it prefers shallow water or very wet mud, kingcup will tolerate occasional depths of up to 15cm (6in). 'Flore Pleno' has double flowers. Kingcup looks best in an informal or wildlife pond or a natural stream. Division: early spring or late summer.

Cotula coronopifolia
Golden buttons
○ ❖ SUMMER
H 15cm (6in), **S** 30cm (12in)

Button-like, bright yellow flowers are the main attraction of this low-growing perennial, but it also comes with leaves that are strongly aromatic when crushed. Looking best in an informal pond, it has creeping growth and spreads slowly to form a good clump. Grow it in water up to 10cm (4in) deep. Division: autumn.

Cyperus longus Sweet galingale
○ ◑ e⁺ ❖ LATE SUMMER to EARLY AUTUMN
H to 1.5m (5ft), **S** 1m (40in) or more

Most cyperus like wet or boggy conditions and are vigorous spreaders. Sweet galingale is one of the best known and most suitable for gardens. It has stiff, long, narrow, grass-like leaves, with thick central ribs. Slim, triangular stems topped with a ruff of leaves and heads of red-brown, rush-like flowers appear from late summer. Plant it in water 8–15cm (3–6in) deep, in a semi-formal or formal pond. Division: spring.

Equisetum hyemale Scouring rush
○ ◑ e⁺ ❖ YEAR-ROUND
H to 1.2m (4ft), **S** 20cm (8in) or more

Horsetails are generally to be avoided in gardens because they are invasive plants with deep roots, impossible to eradicate. However, scouring rush is one that is suitable for a larger pond, where it will flourish in water about 5cm (2in) deep. It has evergreen cylindrical stems marked with dark bands, and no leaves. The stem-tops have a brown tuft containing spores. Plant it in a container to keep it in check. Division: summer.

Eriophorum angustifolium
Cotton grass
○ pH↓ e⁺ ❖ SUMMER
H 30–45cm (12–18in), **S** 30cm (12in) or more

A clear warning of boggy ground in high moorland places, cotton grass has distinctive tufted heads of white, feathery-hairy flowers that look like pieces of cotton wool caught on long, slim stems. The leaves are slender and drooping with sharp, pointed ends. It thrives in shallow water to 5cm (2in) deep and in bog gardens, and also looks good in informal and wildlife ponds. Division: spring.

Glyceria maxima var. variegata
Variegated reed sweet-grass
○ ◑ ❖ MID- to LATE SUMMER
H 80cm (32in), **S** 90cm (3ft) or more

This grassy plant (a variegated form of the native species) has long, strap-shaped leaves that arch elegantly. They are striped green, cream and white, flushed pink when young. The loose, grass-like spikes of flowers may be tinted green or purple. Suiting semi-formal to formal ponds, in water up to 15cm (6in) deep, it is best grown in a container to restrict its spread. Division: early spring.

Houttuynia cordata 'Chameleon'

◐◐ ✤ EARLY to MIDSUMMER
H to 30cm (12in), **S** 45cm (18in)

Relatively short in stature, and suitable for an informal pond, this houttuynia is grown for its colourful foliage, which is variegated pink, yellow, green and white. The leaves are ivy-like and almost heart-shaped at the base, and the leaf-stalks are red-pink. Small white flowers appear in spring. It likes to be in water up to 10cm (4in) deep. Where it is happy, it can spread rapidly, so it is best grown in containers to restrict it to where it is wanted. Division: spring.

Hypericum elodes
Marsh St John's wort

◐◐ e⁺ ✤ SUMMER
H 8–15cm (3–6in), **S** 45cm (18in)

This is a tiny plant with small yellow flowers and rounded bunches of softly hairy, grey-green leaves on lax stems that root as they spread. It can live beside a pond or stream or slightly submerged in up to 8cm (3in) of water, so is good for softening hard edges and disguising liners. It is ideal for an informal or wildlife pond. For more plants, divide in spring.

Iris laevigata Japanese water iris
◐◐ pH↓ ✤ EARLY to MIDSUMMER
H 80cm (32in), **S** 25cm (10in)

The Japanese water iris is an elegant plant with sword-shaped, rich-green leaves and two to four purple-blue flowers on each slim stem in early or midsummer. 'Variegata' (shown above) has cream-striped leaves. Other flower colours include pure white (var. *alba*) and white heavily mottled with blue ('Colchesterensis'). Plant in 10cm (4in) of water. Division: after flowering.

Iris pseudacorus Yellow flag
◐◐ pH↓ e⁺ ✤ MID- to LATE SUMMER
H to 1.5m (5ft), **S** 1m (40in) or more

This native iris is very vigorous and spreads rapidly, so it is best at the side of a large informal or wildlife pond, where it should be kept under control by regular division (midsummer to early autumn). It has long, ribbed, sword-shaped leaves and the flowering stems produce up to 12 yellow flowers with brown or purple markings. Good varieties: 'Alba' (creamy-white flowers); 'Variegata' (striped white and green leaves). In water, plant 15cm (6in) deep.

Iris versicolor American blue flag
◐◐ pH↓ ✤ EARLY to MIDSUMMER
H 30–80cm (12–32in), **S** 25cm (10in)

A smallish iris for smaller ponds, the American blue flag has branched flower stems with up to five blue-violet or lavender-blue flowers with white, vein-like markings. 'Kermesina' has reddish-purple flowers. The leaves of these irises may be slightly arching or upright. Grow in water 10cm (4in) deep. Division: after flowering.

Juncus effusus f. spiralis
Corkscrew rush

◐◐ pH↓ ✤ SUMMER
H 45cm (18in), **S** 60cm (24in)

Perhaps more a curiosity than a thing of beauty, this rush (a form of the native corkscrew rush) has spiralling, dark green stems that form a tangled heap. Its typically rush-like flowers, small and brown, appear along the stems all summer. Plant it where it can be admired close up. It will thrive in boggy ground or in up to 8cm (3in) of water. Division: mid-spring to early summer.

Juncus ensifolius Swordleaf rush
○◐ ❖ SUMMER
H and **S** 30cm (12in)

With leaves rather like those of the irises, but much smaller, this is an attractive little rush that is excellent for smaller water features in water up to 10cm (4in) deep. The leaves are overtopped by round heads of spiky brown flowers in summer. These are long-lasting and in some areas have acquired the imaginative name of flying hedgehogs. Division: mid-spring to early summer.

Lobelia cardinalis Cardinal flower
○◐ ❖ LATE SUMMER to EARLY AUTUMN
H 90cm (3ft), **S** 30cm (12in)

Although not usually recognized as a marginal plant, this tall lobelia grows well in shallow water (10cm/4in), which keeps it safe from slugs. It has glossy, bronze-tinted green leaves that are long and narrow. Its bright red flowers are produced at the stem-tops from late summer. Good varieties with similar colouring: 'Queen Victoria'; 'Bee's Flame' (shown above). Division: spring.

Mentha aquatica Watermint
○e⁺ ❖ SUMMER
H 15–90cm (6–36in), **S** 1m (40in)

There is a mint for any occasion, and this one loves getting its feet wet in water 15cm (6in) deep or in the damp edges of, ideally, an informal or wildlife pond. The small lilac flowers appear in rounded clusters in summer, and its oval leaves are mint-scented when crushed. Its purplish stems root at every opportunity, so grow it in a container to keep it in check and hack it back as necessary.

Menyanthes trifoliata Bog bean
○◐e⁺ ❖ EARLY SUMMER
H 20–30cm (8–12in), **S** 30–50cm (12–20in)

This is a pretty, spreading plant with leaves divided into three rounded leaflets with pointed tips. Glossy and bright green, they are carried on dark stems that emerge from long, dark rhizomes. The pink-tinged, white flowers with fringed petals appear most readily in a sunny spot. Best in a wildlife or informal pond. Plant in water 15–23cm (6–9in) deep. Division: summer.

Mimulus luteus Monkey musk
○◐ ❖ LATE SPRING to SUMMER
H 30cm (12in), **S** 60cm (24in)

Grown for its wide-faced, red-marked yellow flowers, monkey musk is an eye-catching plant for an informal or wildlife pond, where it flourishes in shallow water to 8cm (3in) deep. It has pale green leaves on upright and sprawling stems, good for hiding liners. It self-seeds freely; weed seedlings out or, if you want more plants, pot some up, placing the pot in a tray of water to keep the soil wet, and protect from frost.

Mimulus ringens Allegheny monkey flower, Lavender musk
○◐ ❖ EARLY to LATE SUMMER
H to 1m (40in), **S** 30cm (12in)

This tall, slender, upright mimulus has square stems and narrow, tubular flowers, varying from violet to purple-blue or white, sometimes pink, on stems growing out from the leaf nodes in the upper parts of the plant. The leaves are long, slim and pointed with distinct veins. It is a plant that best suits an informal or wildlife pond. Grow it in water 5–15cm (2–6in) deep and divide in spring to keep it vigorous.

Myosotis scorpioides
Water forget-me-not
○ ◐ e⁺ ❖ EARLY SUMMER
H 15–30cm (6–12in), S 30cm (12in)

Sometimes called *M. palustris*, this is a water-loving relative of the well-known common forget-me-not, with pale blue flowers that have white, yellow or sometimes pink centres. It has angular stems and the hairy leaves are a rich green. Grow it in an informal or wildlife pond in water up to 10cm (4in) deep. It spreads around happily (it can be divided in spring) and may self-seed.

Oenanthe javanica 'Flamingo'
Variegated water dropwort
○ ◐ ❖ SPRING and SUMMER
H 30cm (12in), S 1m (40in)

This marginal is grown for its attractive pale green, celery-like leaves, which have pale pink and white splashes and markings. It also has flat heads of small white flowers in summer. It makes an early appearance in spring, helping to provide interest around the edges of ponds, streams and other water features, where it likes to be in up to 10cm (4in) of water. Trim it to keep it compact. Division: late spring.

Pontederia cordata Pickerel weed
○ ❖ LATE SUMMER
H 60–90cm (2–3ft), S to 75cm (30in)

The striking blue flowers of this marginal or aquatic plant are its most attractive feature. They appear in tightly packed, cylindrical spires in late summer, above the elegant, glossy, heart-shaped, pale green foliage. A large clump looks good in the margins of either a formal or a natural pond, but it will also tolerate water to 30cm (12in) deep. Division: spring or early summer.

Ranunculus flammula
Lesser spearwort
○ ◐ e⁺ ❖ EARLY SUMMER
H 30cm (12in), S 75cm (30in)

A good choice for a natural or wildlife pond, or at the edge of a stream, lesser spearwort has a sprawling, lax habit and bright yellow, buttercup flowers on slender stems in early summer. Its long, narrow leaves are dark green. Grow it with other smaller plants in water up to 15cm (6in) deep. Division: spring.

Ranunculus lingua 'Grandiflorus' Greater spearwort
○ ◐ ❖ EARLY SUMMER
H 60–90cm (2–3ft) or more, S 30–60cm (12–24in)

With delicate yellow, buttercup flowers and long, narrow, bright green leaves, this is an informal, showy plant for a larger pond, including a wildlife pond (this is a form of the native greater spearwort). It can become invasive, so grow it in a container to restrict its spread, ideally in water 15–23cm (6–9in) deep. Division: spring.

Sagittaria sagittifolia 'Flore Pleno' Arrowhead
○ ❖ SUMMER
H to 90cm (3ft), S 30–45cm (12–18in)

This elegant, double-flowered form of the native arrowhead has arrow-shaped leaves on tall stems above the water, while under water the ribbon-like leaves float in the shallows. Even taller stems with fluffy white, pompon flowers appear in summer. Like many marginal plants, it can be over-enthusiastic, so keep it in check by planting it in a container, in water up to 30cm (12in) deep. Division: spring.

Saururus cernuus Lizard's tail
○ ◑ ❖ SUMMER
H 45cm (18in), S to 60cm (24in)
or more

It is worth growing this plant for its striking flowers alone. They are carried in wispy, arching, tail-like spikes above the leaves and are white and scented. The leaves are also attractive, with pointed tips and heart-shaped bases supported on slender, branching stems. Plant it in a container in water to 10cm (4in) deep. Division: spring.

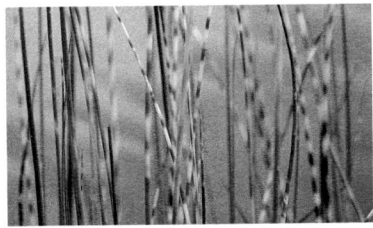

Schoenoplectus lacustris subsp. *tabernaemontani* 'Zebrinus'
Striped club rush
○ ❖ EARLY to LATE SUMMER
H 1m (40in), S 60cm (24in)

Excellent for providing contrast with the arrow-shaped leaves of many marginals, this little club rush (a form of the native species) has cylindrical green stems with heavy white bands from top to bottom. In summer it produces feathery brown flowers at the stem-tips, which add to its decorative charm. Remove any plain green stems. It tolerates water to 30cm (12in) deep. Division: mid-spring.

Typha latifolia 'Variegata'
Variegated reedmace
○ ◑ ❖ SUMMER
H 1.2m (4ft), S indefinite

Suitable for only the largest informal ponds, the variegated form of our native reedmace (commonly known as bulrush) is a striking plant, with strappy, white-striped green leaves and large heads of brown flowers. The flowerheads are thickly cylindrical, topped with a distinct narrow point. They are popular for dried arrangements. Grow this one in water to 40cm (16in) deep; control it by planting in a large container. Division: spring.

Typha minima Dwarf reedmace
○ ◑ ❖ MID- to LATE SUMMER
H 75cm (30in), S to 45cm (18in)

Neat and restrained, this bulrush (as it is often called – strictly speaking, it is a reedmace) provides an eye-catching display in a small formal pond or container. It has narrow leaves, to 30cm (12in) long, and almost rounded brown flowerheads 5cm (2in) long, like tiny floating balloons. It can in survive water up to 15cm (6in) deep. Division: spring.

Veronica beccabunga Brooklime
○ ◑ e⁺ ❖ LATE SPRING to LATE SUMMER
H 10cm (4in), S 45cm (18in) or more

This low-growing plant, which suits an informal or wildlife pond, produces loose heads of blue flowers with white centres throughout the growing season. It has toothed, rounded, fleshy leaves on branching stems that root where they touch the ground. Prevent unwanted spread by trimming back the stems and dividing the plant in summer. It can be grown in water up to 12cm (5in) deep.

Zantedeschia aethiopica Arum lily
○ ❄ ❖ LATE SPRING to MIDSUMMER
H 90cm (3ft), S 60cm (2ft)

Among the most elegant of marginal plants, arum lilies are ideal for formal to semi-formal situations. They have arrow-shaped, glossy, bright green leaves and large flowerheads consisting of a yellow spike surrounded by a white spathe. Grow them in water 20–30cm (8–12in) deep. They are not fully hardy, so protect them from hard winters with a deep mulch or plant them in a container and lift them for winter. Divide in spring. 'Little Gem', 45cm (18in) tall and a prolific flowerer, is less hardy.

Waterside and bog garden plants

If you have an informal pond, it's lovely to extend the watery theme out into the garden, perhaps in the form of a bog garden (*see* pages 42–3). This increases the naturalistic effect and allows you to use some really showy plants. Some thrive in boggy conditions; others tolerate damp but not permanently wet soil (*see* Key, page 71) and are best sited around the edge of the pond or bog garden rather than within it.

Trees and shrubs

Trees are excellent for framing views and providing height around a pond or bog garden, while shrubs create shelter for smaller plants as well as wildlife. The plants featured here will tolerate damp but do not like permanently wet soil, so place them at the water's edge or on mounds raised slightly above ground level. Make sure branches won't overhang the pond (*see* page 24).

Alnus incana 'Aurea' Grey alder
○◑▲ ❖YEAR-ROUND
H 10m (30ft), S 5m (15ft)

Alders are known for their liking for damp soil, but most are too big for the average garden. This one makes a small, upright tree and, to add to its charms, has yellow-gold leaves in spring and, in winter, cone-like fruits and orange shoots bearing orange-red catkins. The leaves are pale green in summer. It will survive in dry soil too, so would also be good planted at a distance from the pond.

Amelanchier lamarckii
Snowy mespilus
○◑▲ ❖SPRING to AUTUMN
H 10m (30ft), S 6m (20ft)

Although it likes reasonable drainage, this lovely, shrubby tree tolerates damp waterside sites. It has delicate white flowers in spring, followed by purple fruits. The leaves open bronze, becoming dark green, then orange and red in autumn. Plant it where its airy habit can make attractive reflections in the water.

Andromeda polifolia
Common bog rosemary
○◑▲ pH↓ ❖SPRING to EARLY SUMMER
H 40cm (16in), S 50–60cm (20–24in)

This very low, sometimes prostrate, evergreen shrub loves a bog garden. Wiry stems hold rosemary-like leaves, and white or pale pink flowers hang from the stem-tips. 'Compacta' (shown above) is just 20cm (8in) tall. 'Blue Ice' has blue-green leaves.

Betula pendula 'Youngii'
Young's weeping birch
○◑▲ ❖YEAR-ROUND
H and S 8m (25ft)

Forming a mound of branches and foliage, this weeping birch should really be grown as a specimen or feature tree where its shape can be fully appreciated, perhaps hanging alongside a pond or stream bank. It has white bark, oval, toothed leaves (green in summer and yellow in autumn) and yellow-brown catkins in spring. Birches tolerate moist ground but also like good drainage, so avoid permanently wet sites.

Cornus alba Red-barked dogwood
○◑▲ ❖YEAR-ROUND
H and S to 2m (6ft)

Cut the stems of *C. alba* to the ground each spring to encourage bright-red new growth for winter interest. They have dense heads of tiny white flowers followed by white, blue-tinted fruits. The leaves are dark green turning orange or red in autumn. 'Kesselringii' has purple-black winter shoots; those of 'Sibirica' (shown above) are bright red. Plant dogwood in a large, waterside clump with low-growing companions so its bright stems can make a real splash.

Cornus sanguinea
Common dogwood
○ ◐ 🌢 ❖ YEAR-ROUND
H 3m (10ft), **S** 2.5m (8ft)

Without annual pruning, this dogwood makes a large, shrubby tree, but with pruning you get the benefit of more brightly coloured, red-green or green shoots in winter. It has flat heads of white flowers in summer and blue-black fruits. 'Midwinter Fire' is widely available; it has flame-coloured winter shoots with orange bases and red-pink tops. Plant cornus at the pond's edge.

Hydrangea macrophylla
Common hydrangea
○ ◐ 🌢 ❖ MID- to LATE SUMMER
H 2m (6ft), **S** 2.5m (8ft)

This has large, oval, pale to dark green leaves and heads of long-lasting flowers, usually blue on acid soils and pink on alkaline. The heads may be flattened (lacecaps) or rounded (mopheads). Varieties include: lacecaps 'Mariesii Perfecta' (shown above), with blue, mauve or pink flowers, and 'Veitchii', with white flowers turning pink with age; the mophead 'Blue Bonnet' has blue or pink flowers.

Salix caprea 'Kilmarnock'
Kilmarnock willow
○ 🌢 ❖ MID- to LATE SPRING
H 1.5–2m (5–6ft), **S** 2m (6ft)

Relishing a dampish position in deep soil, this attractive, weeping tree is a common sight in many urban gardens. Make sure you can accommodate it – perhaps on a mound – without having to prune the long, weeping branches as this spoils its beauty. Grey catkins smothered with yellow anthers appear before the leaves, which are long and dark green, greyish on the underside.

Sorbaria tomentosa var. angustifolia
○ ◐ pH↑🌢 ❖ MID- to LATE SUMMER
H and **S** to 3m (10ft)

This is an attractive, spreading shrub with leaves divided into many narrow, dark green leaflets, giving it a light, airy appearance. The fluffy heads of white flowers open from neat, tiny, round buds. The plant can spread widely by suckers, which appear around the base of the plant; remove these as necessary. Ideal for the edge of a bog garden.

Sorbus aucuparia
Mountain ash, Rowan
○ ◐ pH↓🌢 ❖ SPRING
H 15m (50ft), **S** 7m (22ft)

This is equally lovely as a single tree in a small urban garden or in a wild area in a larger one. Its leaves consist of many dark green, narrow leaflets and in spring it produces heads of white flowers. Orange-red berries follow and are very popular with birds. The leaves turn red or yellow in autumn. It tolerates damp soil, but also appreciates some drainage. 'Sheerwater Seedling' is smaller and narrower (H 10m/30ft, S 5m/15ft).

Viburnum opulus Guelder rose
○ ◐ 🌢 ❖ LATE SPRING and EARLY SUMMER
H 5m (15ft), **S** 4m (12ft)

A native hedgerow plant, the guelder rose tolerates a wide range of conditions, including damp with some drainage. It has maple-like, dark green leaves, usually with three lobes, and flat heads of white flowers, like a lacecap hydrangea. These are followed by clear red, fleshy fruits, appreciated by birds. The leaves turn red in autumn. Guelder rose is ideal in a wild or informal garden.

Brunnera macrophylla
○ ◑ ● ◢ ❖ MID- and LATE SPRING
H 45cm (18in), **S** to 60cm (24in)

This is a pretty little plant for a waterside location. Happy in shade, it produces a clump of large, heart-shaped leaves from which the flowering stem emerges in spring, bearing bright blue, forget-me-not-like flowers and narrow leaves. Good variegated varieties: 'Jack Frost' (white with darker veins; shown above); 'Looking Glass' (silver-white leaves).

Cardamine pratensis
Cuckoo flower, Lady's smock
○ ◑ ❖ LATE SPRING
H to 45cm (18in), **S** 15cm (6in)

A native wildflower, this delicate plant is common in damp meadows and looks like a more refined version of the garden weed hairy bittercress, to which it is related. Long stalks bear heads of small, pale pink flowers with yellow centres. Massed plantings are most effective, particularly at the front of a bog garden where it is not swamped by other plants. 'Flore Pleno' has darker, double flowers.

Carex elata 'Aurea'
Bowles's golden sedge
○ ◑ ❖ LATE SPRING to EARLY SUMMER
H 60–70cm (24–28in), **S** 45cm (18in)

Making an arching, upright clump of wide, bright yellow, grassy leaves, this sedge is an eye-catcher spilling over the edge of water or beside a shady path. It produces long brown spikes of grass-like flowers from late spring, which are attractive *en masse*.

Carex siderosticha 'Variegata'
○ ◑ ❖ LATE SPRING
H 30cm (12in), **S** 40cm (16in)

This sedge is rather like a low-growing bamboo, with wide, strap-shaped, pale green leaves edged with white stripes. The tiny flowers are grass-like and brown, but are not the reason for growing it. Plant this sedge with plants that have contrasting leaves, such as those of the rodgersias (*see* page 91), or plant it in a large group for impact in any waterside or boggy spot.

Cornus canadensis
Creeping dogwood
○ ◑ pH↓◢ ❖ LATE SPRING to EARLY SUMMER
H 15cm (6in), **S** indefinite

A very wide-spreading, low-growing plant that is suitable for ground cover in a damp spot, creeping dogwood is also quite showy. It has short stems with whorls of pointed oval leaves. The white flowerheads appear on top of these in spring and are followed by bright red berries in autumn. Plant it somewhere near to water where it has room to make an extravagant clump and remove excess growth as necessary.

Darmera peltata
○ ◑ ❖ LATE SPRING
H 2m (6ft), **S** 1m (40in)

This is an impressive foliage plant for boggy soil. Its huge, rounded leaves, up to 30cm (12in) across, are glossy dark green in summer and turn red in autumn. In spring, flower stalks 2m (6ft) tall rise above them, bearing rounded heads of bright pink or white flowers. This is a plant that does need space to look its best, but as it is slow to spread, it is not usually a problem.

Cornus sanguinea
Common dogwood
◯ ◑ 🌢 ❖ YEAR-ROUND
H 3m (10ft), S 2.5m (8ft)

Without annual pruning, this dogwood makes a large, shrubby tree, but with pruning you get the benefit of more brightly coloured, red-green or green shoots in winter. It has flat heads of white flowers in summer and blue-black fruits. 'Midwinter Fire' is widely available; it has flame-coloured winter shoots with orange bases and red-pink tops. Plant cornus at the pond's edge.

Hydrangea macrophylla
Common hydrangea
◯ ◑ 🌢 ❖ MID- to LATE SUMMER
H 2m (6ft), S 2.5m (8ft)

This has large, oval, pale to dark green leaves and heads of long-lasting flowers, usually blue on acid soils and pink on alkaline. The heads may be flattened (lacecaps) or rounded (mopheads). Varieties include: lacecaps 'Mariesii Perfecta' (shown above), with blue, mauve or pink flowers, and 'Veitchii', with white flowers turning pink with age; the mophead 'Blue Bonnet' has blue or pink flowers.

Salix caprea 'Kilmarnock'
Kilmarnock willow
◯ 🌢 ❖ MID- to LATE SPRING
H 1.5–2m (5–6ft), S 2m (6ft)

Relishing a dampish position in deep soil, this attractive, weeping tree is a common sight in many urban gardens. Make sure you can accommodate it – perhaps on a mound – without having to prune the long, weeping branches as this spoils its beauty. Grey catkins smothered with yellow anthers appear before the leaves, which are long and dark green, greyish on the underside.

Sorbaria tomentosa var. angustifolia
◯ ◑ pH↑🌢 ❖ MID- to LATE SUMMER
H and S to 3m (10ft)

This is an attractive, spreading shrub with leaves divided into many narrow, dark green leaflets, giving it a light, airy appearance. The fluffy heads of white flowers open from neat, tiny, round buds. The plant can spread widely by suckers, which appear around the base of the plant; remove these as necessary. Ideal for the edge of a bog garden.

Sorbus aucuparia
Mountain ash, Rowan
◯ ◑ pH↓🌢 ❖ SPRING
H 15m (50ft), S 7m (22ft)

This is equally lovely as a single tree in a small urban garden or in a wild area in a larger one. Its leaves consist of many dark green, narrow leaflets and in spring it produces heads of white flowers. Orange-red berries follow and are very popular with birds. The leaves turn red or yellow in autumn. It tolerates damp soil, but also appreciates some drainage. 'Sheerwater Seedling' is smaller and narrower (H 10m/30ft, S 5m/15ft).

Viburnum opulus Guelder rose
◯ ◑ 🌢 ❖ LATE SPRING and EARLY SUMMER
H 5m (15ft), S 4m (12ft)

A native hedgerow plant, the guelder rose tolerates a wide range of conditions, including damp with some drainage. It has maple-like, dark green leaves, usually with three lobes, and flat heads of white flowers, like a lacecap hydrangea. These are followed by clear red, fleshy fruits, appreciated by birds. The leaves turn red in autumn. Guelder rose is ideal in a wild or informal garden.

Bulbs

Most bulbs (including rhizomes) like hot, dry conditions in summer, but those shown here are happy in moist soil near a pond or stream, where they will reward with lots of flowers and lush foliage. If flowers become sparse after a few years, lift and divide the plants after flowering. Plant in groups for the most impact and a natural effect.

Fritillaria meleagris
Snakeshead fritillary
○ ◑ ◢ ❖ SPRING

H 25–30cm (10–12in), S to 8cm (3in)

At its very best planted *en masse* in a damp meadow, snakeshead fritillary also looks good among primroses, anemones and other spring flowers in shady, moist soil. The bell-shaped flowers – purple or mauve with darker check, or sometimes white – hang from slender stems. Leaves are narrow, dark green and glossy.

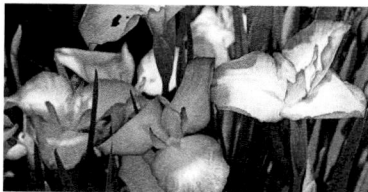

Iris ensata
○ ◑ pH↓ ◢ ❖ MIDSUMMER

H 90cm (3ft), S 25cm (10in)

A relative of *I. laevigata* (*see* page 78), this plant likes a slightly less watery site, but is lovely near water. In midsummer stems bear three or four purple or red-purple flowers up to 15cm (6in) across. The many varieties include two white ones: 'Moonlight Waves', with green centres; 'Gracieuse' with purple edges (shown above).

Iris sibirica Siberian iris
○ ◑ ◢ ❖ EARLY SUMMER

H to 1.2m (4ft), S 30cm (12in)

This elegant iris is perfect beside water, where it tolerates both damp and dryish soil. It has narrow, grassy leaves and branched stems of up to five flowers to 7cm (3in) across. The blue-violet species is a parent of many other irises, including the pale blue 'Sky Wings', yellow and white 'Butter and Sugar' (shown above) and white *I.* 'Sibirica Alba'.

Leucojum aestivum
Summer snowflake
○ ◢ ❖ SUMMER

H to 60cm (24in), S 8cm (3in)

Summer snowflake has slender stems of dainty, white, bell-shaped flowers – like big snowdrops – in summer and wide, strappy leaves. Shown above is 'Gravetye Giant'. It is best in large clumps near water, or under shrubs and trees beside water. *L. vernum* is similar but flowers in spring. Grow both for a long display.

Narcissus bulbocodium
Hoop petticoat daffodil
○ ◢ ❖ MID-SPRING

H to 15cm (6in), S 8cm (3in)

This is an unusual-looking daffodil, with dainty yellow, wide-open trumpet flowers, each with a ruff of thin petals. The dark green leaves are narrow and grassy. Grow it close to the pond, where its unusual flowers can be appreciated and it will not be swamped by more vigorous bog-loving plants.

Schizostylis coccinea Kaffir lily
○ ◢ ❖ AUTUMN

H to 60cm (24in), S 20cm (8in)

This plant (also called *Hesperantha coccinea*) forms clumps of more or less evergreen, narrowly sword-shaped, pale green leaves among which stems of star-shaped scarlet flowers appear in autumn. Growing in a warm spot with shelter from cold winds, it will spread quite widely. Good varieties: 'Major' (large, red; shown above); 'Sunrise' (rich pink); 'Viscountess Byng' (pale pink, late autumn). Looking good by a stream, rill or pond, kaffir lilies will also enjoy a sheltered spot alongside a wall spout.

Perennials

As is often the case elsewhere in the garden, perennials are the mainstay of the bog garden and other damp areas. They have such a wide variety of shapes, colours and textures that there is something for every spot and every taste. When selecting plants, focus on foliage and form rather than just the blooms, since these will be around much longer than the flowers. Divide plants when flowering starts to diminish or clumps get too big (*see* pages 62–3).

Ajuga reptans Bugle
○ ◑ ◮ ❖ SPRING

H 15cm (6in), S 90cm (3ft) or more

This low, wide-spreading evergreen perennial makes excellent ground cover among other more restrained plants, but it also looks good if allowed to form an uninterrupted carpet at the front of a bog garden or beside a pond. It has loose rosettes of oblong, dark green or purple leaves and, in spring, spikes of blue flowers. Dig it up where it is not required. Good varieties: 'Catlin's Giant' (large bronze-purple leaves, flower spikes 20cm/8in; shown above); 'Multicolor' (dark leaves blotched pink and cream); 'Pink Elf' (pink flowers).

Aruncus dioicus Goat's beard
○ ◑ ◮ ❖ EARLY to MIDSUMMER

H 2m (6ft), S 1.2m (4ft)

If you want a plant with impact and long-lasting interest, but don't have room for a shrub, choose goat's beard. It produces large mounds of pale green foliage and tall plumes of tiny white flowers, which continue to look good when brown and faded into autumn. It is a big plant, but very slow to spread. Plant it beside a pond or stream or at the edge of a bog garden.

Asplenium scolopendrium Hart's tongue fern
◑ ◮ ❖ YEAR-ROUND

H to 70cm (28in), S 60cm (24in)

This is an attractive evergreen fern with long, narrow, leathery bright green leaves that often have slightly wavy edges. The leaf-stalk is brown and shiny. The leaves grow in a shuttlecock-like group. This native fern needs good drainage in a moist site and loves a damp bank beside a pond or stream, or even a shady wall. It looks wonderful beside a wall spout or waterfall.

Astilbe
○ ◑ ❖ LATE SPRING to SUMMER

H to 1m (40in), S to 60cm (24in)

The astilbes are an attractive bunch of plants with divided, ferny foliage, above which rise plumes of often brightly coloured, long-lasting flowers. They come in a wide range of shades. Good varieties: 'Fanal' (red, early summer; shown above); 'Irrlicht' (white, late spring to early summer); 'Rheinland' (rich pink); 'Sprite' (pale pink and wispy). Plant a large clump in a bog garden.

Astilboides tabularis
◑ ◮ ❖ EARLY to MIDSUMMER

H 1.5m (5ft), S 1.2m (4ft)

This large-leaved plant is best as an architectural specimen in the shade beside a big pond or a stream in a large garden. Give it plenty of space to show off its large, light green leaves. Its flowers are tiny but carried in large, showy heads above the foliage. Although it likes moisture, it prefers not to be permanently waterlogged.

Brunnera macrophylla

○ ◐ ● ◈ ❖ MID- and LATE SPRING

H 45cm (18in), S to 60cm (24in)

This is a pretty little plant for a waterside location. Happy in shade, it produces a clump of large, heart-shaped leaves from which the flowering stem emerges in spring, bearing bright blue, forget-me-not-like flowers and narrow leaves. Good variegated varieties: 'Jack Frost' (white with darker veins; shown above); 'Looking Glass' (silver-white leaves).

Cardamine pratensis

Cuckoo flower, Lady's smock

○ ◐ ❖ LATE SPRING

H to 45cm (18in), S 15cm (6in)

A native wildflower, this delicate plant is common in damp meadows and looks like a more refined version of the garden weed hairy bittercress, to which it is related. Long stalks bear heads of small, pale pink flowers with yellow centres. Massed plantings are most effective, particularly at the front of a bog garden where it is not swamped by other plants. 'Flore Pleno' has darker, double flowers.

Carex elata 'Aurea'

Bowles's golden sedge

○ ◐ ❖ LATE SPRING to EARLY SUMMER

H 60–70cm (24–28in), S 45cm (18in)

Making an arching, upright clump of wide, bright yellow, grassy leaves, this sedge is an eye-catcher spilling over the edge of water or beside a shady path. It produces long brown spikes of grass-like flowers from late spring, which are attractive *en masse*.

Carex siderosticha 'Variegata'

○ ◐ ❖ LATE SPRING

H 30cm (12in), S 40cm (16in)

This sedge is rather like a low-growing bamboo, with wide, strap-shaped, pale green leaves edged with white stripes. The tiny flowers are grass-like and brown, but are not the reason for growing it. Plant this sedge with plants that have contrasting leaves, such as those of the rodgersias (*see* page 91), or plant it in a large group for impact in any waterside or boggy spot.

Cornus canadensis

Creeping dogwood

○ ◐ pH↓ ◈ ❖ LATE SPRING to EARLY SUMMER

H 15cm (6in), S indefinite

A very wide-spreading, low-growing plant that is suitable for ground cover in a damp spot, creeping dogwood is also quite showy. It has short stems with whorls of pointed oval leaves. The white flowerheads appear on top of these in spring and are followed by bright red berries in autumn. Plant it somewhere near to water where it has room to make an extravagant clump and remove excess growth as necessary.

Darmera peltata

○ ◐ ❖ LATE SPRING

H 2m (6ft), S 1m (40in)

This is an impressive foliage plant for boggy soil. Its huge, rounded leaves, up to 30cm (12in) across, are glossy dark green in summer and turn red in autumn. In spring, flower stalks 2m (6ft) tall rise above them, bearing rounded heads of bright pink or white flowers. This is a plant that does need space to look its best, but as it is slow to spread, it is not usually a problem.

Eupatorium maculatum Atropurpureum Group
Hemp agrimony
○ ◑ ⚘ ❖ SUMMER

H to 2m (6ft), **S** 1m (40in)

Best grown as a background plant because of its huge size, this is a statuesque addition to the side of a pond. Its strong purple stems carry whorls of oval, dark green leaves. At the top of these, large clusters of tiny flowers appear in summer. They are deep rose-purple and very attractive to bees. This plant spreads slowly but self-seeds freely; remove unwanted seedlings.

Filipendula rubra 'Venusta'
○ ◑ ❖ EARLY to MIDSUMMER

H to 2.5m (8ft), **S** 1.2m (4ft)

A splendid plant for a large space, or to take the place of a tree or shrub in a small garden, *F. rubra* is aptly named queen of the prairies. Tall stems carry deeply cut mid-green leaves and fluffy heads of tiny, fragrant flowers (in 'Venusta', rose-pink becoming paler). Remove unwanted growth as necessary. *F. ulmaria* (meadowsweet) is smaller (H to 90cm/3ft), with creamy-white flowers. *F. rubra* and *F. ulmaria* suit an informal damp meadow or bog garden.

Geum rivale Water avens
○ ⚘ ❖ LATE SPRING to MIDSUMMER

H and **S** to 60cm (24in)

Water avens is a pretty little plant with nodding, bell-shaped flowers carried on long stems above the rich-green foliage. In the species, the flowers may be pink or dark orange-red with brown sepals. Good varieties: 'Album' (greenish-white); 'Leonard's Variety' (copper-pink on dark stems, mid- to late summer; shown above); 'Marmalade' (apricot-orange with dark stems). Plant water avens beside a stream or natural pond.

Gunnera magellanica
○ ◑ ❖ SUMMER

H 15cm (6in), **S** 30cm (12in) or more

This diminutive plant forms a bright green, glossy mat. The scalloped edges of its small leaves are raised, making a bowl, while short stalks carry panicles of tiny green flowers that are followed by orange-red fruits. *G. magellanica* is related to *G. manicata*, famed for its enormous leaves to 2m (6ft) long and not suitable for the average-sized garden. Gunneras need permanently wet soil, making good ground cover in a bog garden or on the banks of a stream.

Heloniopsis orientalis
◑ pH↓⚘ ❖ LATE SPRING to EARLY SUMMER

H and **S** to 20cm (8in)

This is an unusual perennial with heads of pendent, starry, rose-pink flowers with long stamens and styles, atop thick, dark red flower stems. These rise from a dense mass of large, pale green, leathery evergreen leaves, strap-shaped and sometimes rather floppy. The plant prefers a cool, moist spot; position it where you can appreciate its unusual flowers, perhaps near a pondside seat.

Hemerocallis Day lily
○ ⚘ ❖ SUMMER

H to 75cm (30in) or more, **S** to 60cm (24in) or more

Most day lilies produce clumps of long, strap-shaped leaves, evergreen in some varieties. The flower stems bear clusters of buds that open one or two at a time over a long period, but each flower lasts only a day or so. The flowers range from star-shaped to nearly circular; some are fragrant. Good varieties: 'American Revolution' (rich dark red, evergreen; shown above); 'Catherine Woodbery' (lavender); 'Corky' (yellow, evergreen, tolerates part shade); 'Pandora's Box' (pale cream with a red eye, evergreen).

Heuchera Coral flower
○ ◐ ◑ ✿ SPRING to AUTUMN

H to 60cm (24in), S 45cm (18in)

Heucheras are grown for their colourful leaves, attractive over a long season (and evergreen in some varieties), but they also have slender stems of dainty flowers in spring or summer. The heart-shaped leaves come in a range of colours to suit any scheme. Good varieties: 'Crème Brûlée' (copper, amber; shown above); 'Lipstick' (rich-green with red flowers); 'Plum Pudding' (dark burgundy). They will sit happily with contrasting, upright plants in a waterside setting.

Hosta 'Sum and Substance'
○ ◐ ◑ ✿ MID- to LATE SUMMER

H 75cm (30in), S 1.2m (4ft)

There are literally hundreds of varieties of hosta and all are great at the edge of a bog garden, with a little drainage and shelter from cold winds. Making a large, eye-catching clump, this is one of the biggest varieties, with glossy, heart-shaped, yellow-green leaves, up to 50cm (20in) long. Its flower stems may reach 1m (40in) and carry spikes of very pale, lilac-blue flowers. Hostas also look good in pots near small water features.

Ligularia dentata 'Desdemona'
○ ◐ ✿ MIDSUMMER to EARLY AUTUMN

H and S 1m (40in)

This sturdy, thick-stemmed, perhaps rather coarse-looking plant, produces large, daisy-like flowerheads in dark orange with long ray petals. Its rounded leaves are brown-tinted green with purple undersides and serrated edges. Grow it in the middle of a bog garden or damp border, preferably in a sheltered spot, with something that can hold its own, such as Eupatorium or Darmera.

Ligularia przewalskii
○ ◐ ✿ MID- to LATE SUMMER

H to 2m (6ft), S 1m (40in)

Much more elegant than L. dentata (above), this large, clump-forming perennial has rounded, deeply toothed leaves that contrast well with the dark stems bearing dense spires of yellow flowerheads in mid- and late summer. It suits a tamer setting too, perhaps as a companion to a large hosta or Rodgersia in moist soil. It will also be happy in a bog garden. Give it shelter from wind.

Lychnis chalcedonica
Maltese cross
○ ◐ ◑ ✿ EARLY to MIDSUMMER

H to 1.2m (4ft), S 30cm (12in)

With its rounded heads of bright red to red-orange flowers atop tall stems, this is an eye-catching plant for a damp spot beside a pond. Grow it in large clumps for the best effect. The stems are straight and unbranched, giving the plant a solid appearance, but they do need staking because of the top-heavy blooms. The oval leaves wrap around the stems. Good varieties: 'Alba' (white); 'Carnea' (pale salmon-pink).

Lychnis viscaria German catchfly
○ ◐ ◑ ✿ EARLY to MIDSUMMER

H and S 45cm (18in)

This is a little plant making a clump of dark green, lance-shaped leaves. The sticky flowering stems rise above this, producing star-shaped, purple-pink flowers in great quantities from early summer. The plants often have quite a distinct shape, spreading out from their base in a neat cone shape, which means they look good in groups or singly alongside any water feature.

Lysichiton americanus
Skunk cabbage
○ ◑ ❖ EARLY SPRING
H to 1m (40in), S to 1.2m (4ft)

With large, shiny, oval leaves and pencil-like flower spike surrounded by a large, clear yellow spathe, to 40cm (16in) long, skunk cabbage is a striking plant for any bog garden. The rather unfortunate common name refers to the musky smell of the flowers. For a smaller space, try *L. camtschatcensis*, which has white spathes (H and S 75cm/30in).

Lysimachia clethroides
Gooseneck loosestrife
○ ◑ ◢ ❖ MID- to LATE SUMMER
H 1m (40in), S 60cm (24in)

Clumps of this loosestrife are an attractive sight in a shady spot beside a pond or stream. It has pointed, oval, pale green leaves on strong stems that also produce white flowers at their tips. The flowerheads look similar to those of a buddleia, but are more tapering at their tips. They arch over, straightening up as the flowers open. Unlike many lysimachias, this species is not overly invasive, but dig out growth where it is not wanted.

Lythrum salicaria
Purple loosestrife
○ ❖ MIDSUMMER to EARLY AUTUMN
H 1.2m (4ft), S 90cm (3ft)

With its tall spikes, to 45cm (18in) long, of bright purple-red, starry flowers, this plant is great for a bog garden or in damp soil around a pond. It has stiff, strong stems, perfectly able to support the flowers, with narrow, lance-shaped, softly hairy leaves. 'Feuerkerze' (shown above) has richer, redder flowers, and being slightly shorter (90cm/3ft) is more suited to smaller gardens.

Lythrum virgatum
European wand loosestrife
○ ❖ EARLY to LATE SUMMER
H 90cm (3ft), S 45cm (18in)

This is a tall, slender loosestrife with masses of red-purple flowers all summer, the spikes held on upright stems above dark green leaves. As well as being elegant and eye-catching, the flowers are popular with bees. Good varieties: 'Rose Queen' (bright rose; 60cm/24in); 'The Rocket' (deep pink; H to 80cm/32in; shown above). Plant it in the middle or at the back of a damp border.

Matteuccia struthiopteris
Shuttlecock fern
◑ pH↓ ◢ ❖ SUMMER
H 1.5m (5ft) or more, S 1m (40in)

Aptly named, this fern produces neat, upright shuttlecocks of bright green fronds, typically ferny in appearance. It sends out rhizomes (swollen stems), which run underground to produce the next shuttlecock a short distance away, so an established plant will spread – but it will be a neat, formal-looking colony. Perfect for a shady area at the edge of a pond. Protect from drying winds.

Molinia caerulea
Purple moor grass
○ ◑ pH↓ ◢ ❖ SPRING to AUTUMN
H to 1.5m (5ft), S to 40cm (16in)

This lovely grass is grown for its long, slim yellow flower spikes, which appear early in the year and look good well into autumn. They fan out from the grassy base and have loose, airy flowerheads. Good varieties: subsp. *arundinacea* 'Karl Foerster' (purple flower spikes); subsp. *caerulea* 'Variegata' (dark green and cream leaves, dark yellow stems of purple flowerheads, H to 60cm/2ft; shown above). Ideal for the pondside.

Onoclea sensibilis Sensitive fern
◑ pH↓ 🌢❖ SUMMER

H to 60cm (2ft), **S** indefinite

The sensitive fern (so called because it dies back at the first frost) is a robust-looking plant. In spring, the new fronds are bright green, sometimes bronze; in summer, brown fertile fronds appear with dark, bead-like clusters of spores. It is not a neat grower and spreads around freely, but it creates effective and attractive ground cover. Dig up any unwanted clumps. Grow at the edge of a bog garden or beside a stream.

Osmunda regalis Royal fern
○ ◑ pH↓ ❖ SUMMER

H 2m (6ft), **S** 4m (12ft)

Although capable of great size, in gardens the royal fern is unlikely to become overwhelmingly large. It has bright green, fern-like leaves that are divided into many leaflets. The curious 'flowerheads' appear in summer. Brown-red and stiffly upright, they consist of many small, spore-bearing spikes. It is happy in sun or partial shade, but if you grow it in the sun it needs permanently moist soil. This fern makes a splendid feature plant, by a pond or stream or below a wall spout.

Primula

Choosing primulas

Not all primulas tolerate damp or poorly drained soil, but those that do make an invaluable contribution to a water garden, whether formal or informal in style. They usually have flamboyant flowers on long, slender stalks and look particularly splendid grown in drifts beside still or flowing water. Their leaves are generally similar to those of our native primrose (*Primula vulgaris*), but sometimes quite a lot bigger, and die down in winter. The flowers usually have wide, flat faces, often with a yellow or pale centre, opening out from a narrow tube, which can be long or short. They come in a wide range of colours, from subtle yellows, white and lavender to vivid cerise, pink and orange, and are produced from early or mid-spring into summer.

Some of the primulas that can be grown in a damp position fall into one of two recognizable groups: candelabras and drumsticks. Candelabra primulas have tall stems carrying groups of flowers in separated whorls around the stem. Drumstick primulas have rounded heads of flowers at the top of a stocky stem. Other damp-loving primulas do not belong to either of these groups.

Growing primulas

When buying primulas, do check that they are suitable for your needs, as some must be grown in very well-drained soil or even under cover. Grow moisture-loving primulas (described here) in sun or partial shade, in deep soil with plenty of organic matter. Most prefer damp rather than boggy conditions, and some prefer acid soil. After planting,

Primula japonica is one of the most readily available of all primulas.

primulas grow happily with very little intervention, as long as they are not allowed to dry out in hot, dry spells.

Propagate by dividing clumps from autumn to early spring, while the plants are dormant, or sow seed in early spring.

GOOD PRIMULAS

Primula alpicola – Heads of pendent, scented flowers in white, yellow or violet; needs acid soil; H 50cm (20in).

P. bulleyana – Candelabra type, with crimson flowers ageing orange; needs acid soil; H 60cm (24in).

P. chionantha – One or more whorls of scented white flowers; H 60cm (24in).

P. denticulata – Drumstick type, with pale to mid-purple or white flowers; H 45cm (18in).

P. florindae – Heads of up to 40 drooping, clear yellow fragrant flowers; H to 1.2m (4ft).

P. 'Inverewe' – Candelabra type, with rich-red flowers; prefers neutral to acid soil; H to 75cm (30in).

P. japonica (*see* above)– Whorls carrying up to 25 red-purple, sometimes white flowers; needs acid soil; H 45cm (18in).

P. pulverulenta – Candelabra type, with dark red or purple-red flowers; needs acid soil; H to 1m (40in).

P. vialii – Short-lived but stunning in bloom, with spikes of red buds opening to pale violet-blue flowers; needs acid soil; H to 60cm (24in).

Persicaria affinis

○ ◐ ✿ MIDSUMMER to MID-AUTUMN

H to 25cm (10in), **S** 60cm (24in)

This low-growing, spreading evergreen plant makes dense mats of dark green leaves, which turn red-brown in autumn. Spikes of flowers open dark pink-red and fade to pale pink, so you will see a mix of colours over the long flowering season. Good varieties: 'Darjeeling Red' (pink flowers turning red; shown above); 'Superba' (pale pink flowers becoming red). Persicaria looks good by a stream or waterfall, or among rocks and stones.

Primula beesiana

◐ pH↓ ✿ SUMMER

H and **S** to 60cm (2ft)

This candelabra primula (*see* panel, opposite) produces elegant, long-stemmed, red-pink flowers with yellow eyes in summer. The stems are dusted with a silvery-white, flour-like powder, producing an interesting contrast to the flowers. The leaves, produced at the base of the plant, are typically primrose-shaped but with red midribs, and may be evergreen. In a sunny spot, this primula needs soil that never dries out.

Rheum palmatum 'Atrosanguineum'

Chinese rhubarb

○ ◐ ✿ EARLY SUMMER

H to 2.5m (8ft), **S** 2m (6ft)

A massive plant that looks wonderful near a big natural pond, this ornamental rhubarb needs plenty of space. It is grown for its deeply cut leaves, to 90cm (3ft) long, coloured red when young, turning deep green with purple undersides, and the equally striking, tall vivid-pink flowerheads. *R.* 'Ace of Hearts' is smaller (H 1.2m/4ft, S 90cm/3ft), with pale pink or white flowers.

Rodgersia pinnata

○ ◐ ✿ MID- to LATE SUMMER

H 1.2m (4ft), **S** 75cm (30in)

This attractive architectural plant has leaves to 90cm (3ft) long with deep veins that give them a beautifully textured, almost metallic appearance. They are carried on red-green stems, as are the flowerheads, which tower above them. These are like tall, pointed cones and carry tiny, star-shaped flowers that may be yellow-white, pink or red. This is a fine feature plant for a boggy or damp border. Shown above is 'Superba'.

Rodgersia podophylla

○ ◐ ✿ MID- to LATE SUMMER

H to 1.5m (5ft), **S** to 2m (6ft)

The huge leaves of this rodgersia can be up to 40cm (16in) across. They have jagged edges and are heavily textured and purple-bronze when young, becoming dark green and glossy as they mature and redder in autumn. The tiny, creamy-green flowers are star-shaped and carried in loose, many-branched heads on 1.5m (5ft) stems. A really striking plant for the water's edge.

Trollius × cultorum 'Alabaster'

Globeflower

○ ◐ ✿ MID-SPRING to MIDSUMMER

H 60cm (24in), **S** 45cm (18in)

Globeflowers are related to buttercups and have similar, but glossy leaves. Above the foliage, tall stems carry cup-shaped, many-petalled flowers, creamy-white in 'Alabaster'. *T. europaeus* is taller (H 80cm/32in) and slightly less refined, with butter-yellow flowers opening in early spring. Globeflowers are ideal plants for the edge of a bog garden or beside water.

Acknowledgements

BBC Books and OutHouse would like to thank the following for their assistance in preparing this book: Ian Foulkes of Romsey World of Water, Anna Robinson and James Knock of Wayside Aquatics for advice and guidance; Robin Whitecross for picture research; Lesley Riley for proofreading; Marie Lorimer for the index.

Picture credits

Key t = top, b = bottom, l = left, r = right, c = centre

PHOTOGRAPHS

All photographs by Jonathan Buckley except those listed below.

Devon Pond Plants 74bl, 74br

GAP Photos Lee Avison 69t, 77bc; BBC Magazines Ltd 72br; Dave Bevan 82tc, 84bl; Richard Bloom 81tc; Mark Bolton 58t; Elke Borkowski 2/3, 49, 53; Christa Brand 47; Nicola Browne 61b; Rachel Chappell 82tr; Sarah Cuttle 55t, 75br; Maayke de Ridder 89br; Paul Debois 89tc; Carole Drake 42t & b, 76tc, 79bl, 86bc, 87bc; Geoff du Feu 39; Ron Evans 16br; FhF Greenmedia 46b, 71tr; Suzie Gibbons 38; John Glover 14(1), 19br, 50, 82bc, 88tc, 91bc; Jerry Harpur 16bl; Marcus Harpur 81bl; Neil Holmes 87tc; Michael Howes 68l; Martin Hughes-Jones 83bc, tc & tr, 86tr, 91tl & br; Janet Johnson 58b, 69b; Andrea Jones 85br; Lynn Keddie 51, 78tr, 88br; Fiona Lea 12, 44t, 88tl; Fiona McLeod 54b; Clive Nichols 15(2), 21t; Brian North 31; Hanneke Reijbroek 14(2); Howard Rice 71tl, 73l, 77bl, 77tc, 77br; S & O 90b &tr; J S Sira 77tr, 81tl; Martin Staffler 48; Friedrich Strauss 74bc; Visions 73bc, 74tc, 74tr, 75tc, 75bc, 76br, 76l, 79tl, 80br; Juliette Wade 18t; Mel Watson 89tl; Jo Whitworth 89bl; Rob Whitworth 87bl; Mark Winwood 29; Dave Zubraski 81bc

Garden Collection Liz Eddison 13, 18b, 21b, 22(2), 23(2), 26; John Glover 20t; Derek Harris 4, 17t; Andrew Lawson 44t, 55b, 59b; Marie O'Hara 22(1); Gary Rogers 46t; Derek St Romaine 24b; Nicola Stocken Tomkins 20bl, 23(1), 34t; Neil Sutherland 17b

Garden Picture Library/Getty Images Carole Drake 41(1)

Garden World Images Dave Bevan 67r.2, 76bc, 80tc; Lola Claeys Bouuaert 16t; N+R Colborn 82l; Tony Cooper 10t; Gilles Delacroix 78br; Graham Elkington 79br; Frank Emonds 79tc; Steffen Hauser 71bl; Andrea Jones 14(3); MAP/Nathalie Pasquel 37; John Martin 64b, 87tr; Mein Schoener Garten 61t; Ellen McKnight 73tr; Gary Smith 65t

Sue Gordon 62t & b, 64t, 75tr, 78tc

iStockphoto Andrew Howe 41(3); Alasdair James 67r.1; Steve McBill 41(4)

Marianne Majerus Garden Images 5l, 5r

Nature Photographers Ltd Richard Revels/NPL 41(2), 67r.4; 73br, 78bl

NHPA 67r.3

Raymond Turner 19bl

Robin Whitecross 24t

Superstock 59(1), (2) & (3), 80tr

UKWildflowers.com 75tl

Wayside Aquatics 73tc, 80bl

ILLUSTRATIONS

Lizzie Harper 56, 66b, c & f

Sue Hillier 66a, d & e, 67a & b

Janet Tanner 32, 35, 37, 38, 40, 43, 45, 47, 48, 49, 50, 51, 52, 53, 57, 63

Thanks are also due to the following designers and owners whose gardens appear in the book:

Clare Agnew (RHS Chelsea Flower Show 2005) 46t; Chris Beardshaw (RHS Chelsea Flower Show 2006) 22r; John Brookes 61b; Frank Cabot 51; The Hon Mr & Mrs Henry Digby 42b; Paul Dyer 44t; Adrian Hallam, Chris Arrowsmith and Nigel Dunnett 81tc; Mike Harvey 37t; Dean Herald/Fleming's Nurseries (RHS Chelsea Flower Show 2006) 26; Jeffery Hewitt (RHS Chelsea Flower Show 2009); Thomas Hoblyn 53; Ada Hofman Gardens, Loozen, Holland 14(1); Jane Hudson & Erik De Maeijer 22(1); Sara Johnson 18t; Barbara Kennington 21t, 15(2); Lanhydrock Water Garden 4; Jackie Knight Landscapes (RHS Tatton Park Flower Show 2008) 17b; Pam Lewis, Sticky Wicket, Dorset 11t; Lilies Water Garden (Hampton Court Palace Flower Show 2005) 34t; Christopher Lloyd, Great Dixter, East Sussex 54t, 72tl; Guy Marshall 18t; Kathy Miller 5r; Phil Nash 24b; Natural & Oriental Water Gardens 23(2); Ulf Nordfjell 16bl; Roger Oates, Long Barn, Herefordshire 19t; Dan Pearson/Gay Search, London 10b; Roger Platt (RHS Chelsea Flower Show 1996) 19br; Charlotte Rowe 5l; Maureen Sawyer 69t; Sue and Wol Staines, Glen Chantry, Essex 15t, 40; Tom Stuart-Smith 52; Whatley Manor, Wiltshire 20br; Christina Williams 91br; Helen Yemm, East Sussex 9; 11

While every effort has been made to trace and acknowledge all copyright holders, the publisher would like to apologize should there be any errors or omissions.